The Seal of BLESSED MARY

BY HONORIUS AUGUSTODUNENSIS

Translated
by Amelia Carr

PEREGRINA PUBLISHING CO.

Toronto, Ontario

Peregrina Translations Series no. 18

ISBN 0–920669–18–2

Illustrations reproduced with
kind permission of
Österreichische Nationalbibliothek (Vienna)

BX
2349
.H66
1991

1991
All rights reserved

Peregrina Publishing Co.
180 Sherwood Avenue
Toronto Ontario M4P 2A8
Canada
416–482–4488

SIGILLUM BEATÆ MARIAE
THE SEAL OF BLESSED MARY

CONTENTS

INTRODUCTION	
Biography	5
The Sigillum	13
The Canticle of Canticles	15
Honorius' Marian Theology	18
Early Manuscript Tradition	22
Conclusion	27
Edition	29
CANTICLE OF CANTICLES	31
SELECT BIBLIOGRAPHY	44
SIGILLUM BEATÆ MARIÆ	47
End Notes	

PLIBER SCDS DE SPONSA AVSTRI· Scilicet DE FILIA BABYLONIS·
PRECEDENS. TRACTATVS.
erat de filia pharaonis. sequens erit de filia babylonis. Iam legati regis p regina austri missi ueniunt. sponsam in camelis cum magno comitatu adducunt. qua filia pharaonis de uineis cū suis comitibus egressa cū magno tripudio excipit cū magno comitu plausu intē plum regis ducēt. hancq; rex regali munificentia dotatā ad p̄paratū conuiuiū introducēt. sē t̄ aplī p ecclā gentium missi. hanc signis et p̄dicationib; ad xp̄i fidē conuertunt. q̄ multitudo fideliū de iudea

Honorius Augustodunensis, *Expositio in Cantica Canticorum*
(Vienna Österreichische National Bibliothek, Codex 942)

INTRODUCTION

The *Sigillum*, or *Seal of Blessed Mary*, was written by the mysterious Honorius Augustodunensis in the early years of the twelfth century. Closely tied to the liturgy of the mediæval church, the *Sigillum* explains the readings for the August 15th Feast of the Assumption of the Virgin: the Gospel story of Mary and Martha in Luke 10:38–42, the praise of Wisdom from Ecclesiasticus 24:11–23, and the Canticle of Canticles, sometimes called the Song of Songs. Although the date and circumstances of its composition remain in dispute, this text appears to be the first to offer an interpretation of the Canticle based solely on Mary. Thus the *Sigillum* marks an expansive moment in the development of Mariology, when the Canticle becomes a source for Marian theology as well as Marian liturgy. In the years after Honorius writes, the Canticle comes to be viewed not merely as a poem whose individual verses might be read in order to praise the Virgin Mary, but as a revelation which must be studied in its entirety in order to comprehend her. In his little textbook, Honorius initiates us into this new theological and mystical understanding.

BIOGRAPHY

Honorius Augustodunensis remains one of the shadowy figures of the twelfth century. During his lifetime, he deliberately sought anonymity. In the preface to the *Elucidarius* he offers an explanation:

> Moreover, I decided to conceal my name, for fear that destructive envy might bid its devotees scorn and neglect a useful work. May the reader, however, pray that it be recorded in heaven, and never be expunged from the book of life.[1]

Scholars must turn detective to glean even a meager

biography from the scanty references in the writings of Honorius. The primary evidence comes from *De luminaribus ecclesiæ,* a handbook on ecclesiastical writers, which concludes with a brief notice by the author. There he states that he is *Honorius Augustodunensis Ecclesiæ presbyter et scholasticus,* priest and teacher. He then lists his twenty-two works in what is probably chronological order. He concludes, "He flourished under Henry V. What author might come after him, posterity will see." [2]

A rough history of the early career of Honorius can be determined from the phrasing of the prologues to his works. These introductions repeat familiar *topoi* (in fact, Honorius begins the *Sigillum* in exactly the same way as does his direct source). Yet small clues emerge even in the formulaic phrases. The first work, the *Elucidarius,* is dedicated to a convent of his "fellow students." [3] In the opening lines of the next—the *Sigillum*—probably these same students thank Honorius for the little book he sent them, but they have another question to pose: can he explain the reason for the readings on the Feast of the Assumption? In the *Inevitabile* Honorius is asked to clarify still another question, the issue of free will left vague in the *Elucidarius.* These anonymous "brothers" are probably those residing in Canterbury, because Honorius' next work, the *Speculum ecclesiæ,* is specifically dedicated to them. [4] Moreover, since in that text we learn that Honorius preached to those brothers "when he resided among them," we presume that Honorius has now departed Canterbury. In his early work, Honorius is closely allied to these English Benedictines. These first treatises depend intimately upon the work of St. Anselm and material circulating in English circles during the first decade of the twelfth century.[5] He is certainly on the continent by 1110. Flint has suggested that he left England around 1103 at the time of Anselm's last exile. If his sojourn in Canterbury was for the purpose of receiving instruction in the scholastic method of Anselm, his school days now are over.

Henceforth, references in the texts accumulate to create the impression that Honorius is living in south Germany, specifically Regensburg. When he writes of contemporary events, he emphasises imperial history. In the *Imago mundi*, he includes a description of Regensburg, interpolating it into an otherwise borrowed passage. In the *Summa totius*, are biographies of Regensburg and Würzburg saints. Honorius' presence in Germany is confirmed by mapping his influences. Most of the early manuscripts of his work survive in English, German, and Austrian libraries, some decorated and clearly highly valued.

One name that appears in the dedications of Honorius' manuscripts is Cuno (or Conon, German: Kuno), who is probably Cuno of Raitenbuch, active patron of reform and monastic letters, abbot of Siegburg in 1105 and Bishop of Regensburg from 1126 through 1132.[6] Cuno probably commissioned the political *Summa gloria* and may have been responsible for Honorius' move to southern Germany. Indeed, the recipients of Honorius' later works can be located in the Regensburg area. A close relationship emerges in letters and a dedication between Honorius and an abbot Christian. Since "Christian" is a rare name in twelfth–century Germany, this man can readily be identified as the abbot of the Irish monastery of St. James (Jakobskirche) from 1132 to 1152.[7] A well–known Irishman from the royal house of Macarthy, Christian visited his homeland twice and did not return from the second journey when he was elected archbishop of Cashel.

No moment of death is recorded for Honorius. One suggestion is the rather late date of *ca.* 1156, derived from the dedication of one of Honorius's last works. The *Expositio in canticum canticorum* is among the later entries in the list found in the *De luminaribus ecclesiæ*, and is dedicated to the successor of Abbot C., who has recently died. If Abbot C. is Christian, as Endres argued, then the completion of this commentary falls into the reign of Abbot Gregory of St. James (1153–85).[8] If scholars accept that Honorius is writing this last great commentary on the Canticle in the 1150s, then they must account for a long working life. They assign the latest possible dates to his other works (the *Elucidarius* in 1110, the others following in the 1120s or 1130s), or interpose lengthy, eremetic silences between the earlier and later products of Honorius career. Unfortunately, this late dating contradicts Honorius' own statement that he "flourished under Henry V," who ruled from 1105 to 1125. It may be that the clues that scholars have used to date Honorius' activity into the 1150s are simply traces of an "Honorian revival." Perhaps while he lived, Abbot Christian was duty bound to maintain the secrecy that Honorius himself so urgently desired, while his successors felt free to circulate his work more freely.

Recently, Flint has established earlier dates for all of Honorius' works. She has proved that his first compositions originated in England, probably before 1103. An early recension of the *Imago mundi* must be placed around 1110. By this reasoning, the dedications to Christian occurred in the 1130s, early in his tenure as abbot. But most key is her conviction that the second commentary on the Canticle is dedicated not to the successor of Abbot C[hristian], but to that of Abbot C[uno], which would displace Honorius' œuvre by nearly twenty years, and allow him to flourish under Henry V.[9] Most important for our purposes, the revised chronology places the composition of the *Sigillum* in the first decade of the twelfth century, when it emerges as the first Marian reading of the Canticle.

With these biographical facts in mind, we might now attempt to unravel the puzzle of his name. The name Honorius points to Italy or Ireland, confirming the suspicion that Honorius was educated in England and associated with a community of Irish monks. Yet there is some evidence that "Honorius" was a name our author adopted at some point, and that he began life as "Heinricus." Certain early copies of *De imago mundi* are attributed to a Henry. An inscription in the earliest manuscript of the *Sigillum* reads: "Belonging to the noble Henry, may his enemies perish." [10] A manuscript preserved at Göttweig lists a fifty titles of books that were donated by Frater Heinricus; twenty of which can definitely be ascribed to Honorius. Could Frater Heinricus be Honorius, himself? Flint has gone so far as to identify Honorius with Heinricus Augustensis Magister, author of a dialogue on music and a canon regular at the Cathedral of Augsburg.[11] Controversies surrounding issues of reform in Augsburg—specifically the appointment of a new bishop in 1096—led to open conflict and dispersion of the cathedral canons in 1101 and 1104. These events may have prompted the young Henry to study in England and eventually to relocate in Regensburg. They would certainly go far to explain Henry's damnation of his enemies and Honorius' passionate involvement in the debates surrounding reform. Political dangers might also explain Honorius' concern for concealment, although conversion to a new life might in itself be motive enough to take on a new name.

The epithet *Augustodunensis* is more opaque. His eighteenth–century editors translated it simply "of Autun," which has proved mistaken, but persistent. No records in that French city mention him or the office of scholasticus. Moreover, the Latin *Augustodunum* for Autun fell out of general use after the ninth century.[12] Even if there is a subtle autunois influence on Honorius political works,[13] it is too slight to indicate that Honorius spent significant time in France. We must certainly reject the notion that Honorius hailed from Autun.

An elaborate argument has been mounted to translate *Augustodunensis* as "of Regensburg." The imperial city on the Danube acquired many names in its long history, and even today uses two, the German Regensburg and the Celtic Ratisbona. Honorius' epithet mixes Celtic (*dunum* for "mount") and Latin (*Augustus* or "emperor") in a way that would have been particularly congenial to an Irish monk. Throughout its long history, Regensburg is most prominently associated with the Empire, beginning with its foundation by Marcus Aurelius and continuing as the Salian emperors took up residence there. The "imperial mount" might be the celebrated site outside the walls of the city where Constantine vanquished the pagans. In 1075, on this same hill, the Irish monk Marianus founded the Weih–Sankt–Peter, which later became a priory of St. James, outside the gates of Regensburg.[14] Unfortunately, the records of this church were destroyed in the wars of the sixteenth century, records which might have confirmed this unusual designation and, perhaps, named Honorius as a resident.

Perhaps Augustodunensis is simply a corruption of *Augustiensis*, "of Augsburg." Honorius claim in the *De luminaribus* to be "priest of the church of Augsburg" would commemorate his ordination, perhaps even position him as an exile in the cause of reform. Augustodunensis also evokes the community of St. Augustine at Canterbury where Honorius stayed with St. Anselm. [15]

It is tempting to read Honorius' place designation as an evocative pen–name, a mark of self–identity in an age which increasingly valued personality. Honorius deliberately created a poetic name which would evoke several places where he passed his life and allude to a Celtic and Latin heritage. If Augustodunensis ultimately helps to reinforce his anonymity, it also marks Honorius as a charismatic individual.

Honorius' writing raises other questions about his vocation. Sometimes he defends the viewpoint of a canon, at other times that of the monk. It is more logical that he would have first held the position of canon. Later, perhaps inspired by reform or by St. Anselm, he must have decided to commit himself to the monastic life. Many manuscripts describe Honorius as a *solitarius*, or *inclusus:* perhaps the courtesy title of "hermit" granted to scholars, the special status of the Irish monks, or a retreat within the monastery. But even the mature Honorius never seems fully dead to the world. As a priest and teacher, Honorius felt drawn to the active life. In one of his latest works, the controversial *De liceat monacis prædicare*, Honorius raised his voice to argue that monks should be allowed to preach. All of his writings seem directed to the religious who is engaged in a broad spectrum of ecclesiastical activities.

Dimly, then, we perceive the bare outlines of Honorius' life. His early years were spent in England, the later ones in southern Germany. At some moment early in his life— perhaps already in England—he made a decision to lead a more cloistered life in the manner of the Irish monks. He continued to write in Bavaria, not only composing new works, but revising the old. His death may have occurred at any time between 1135 and 1156.

If Honorius left England sometime between 1102 and 1110, and was living in Regensburg during the time of Cuno (after 1126) and Christian (after 1132), there are still perhaps two decades of his middle age unaccounted for. Some suggest a sojourn in Siegburg under the protection of Cuno, whose avid interest in monastic reform is paralleled by Honorius' polemic.[16] For those, Augustodunensis is a translation of *"Sigetberg,"* or "mount of victory." Supposedly, it was not until Honorius arrived in Siegburg that he acquired a taste for Marian themes under the tutelage of Rupert of Deutz. But since we now know that the *Sigillum* was composed in England, there is less need to include Siegburg on Honorius' itinerary. Extended visits to Flanders or Burgundy might also be included in his biography, as well as to the Austrian monasteries of Lambach and Göttweig.

So many and so diverse are Honorius' sources that, without clearer evidence, it seems unwise to dismiss Southern's observation that Honorius "was perhaps among the last of an ancient and honourable line of wanderers, the wandering scholar–monks of Ireland."[17] Honorius, like his friend Christian of Regensburg, might even have hailed from Cashel, "the hill of Kings," plausibly translated as Augustodunensis. He arrived into the community of Anselm at a time when relations were never more amiable between Ireland and Canterbury. He continued his wanderings on the Continent where a network of Irish churches had been established in the previous centuries.

Honorius' biography will never be fleshed out to our satisfaction. We are forced to know him in the way that he desired: by his works. His literary activity is preserved in some thirty–two compositions, many of which circulated widely and a handful of which were enormously influential in the twelfth century and later. The dedication of the *Gemma animæ* provides insight into the whole of Honorius's œuvre, for it was composed at the specific request of a community of brothers "desiring instruction but lacking in books."[18] In response to the need of struggling new foundations, Honorius composed manageable summaries of significant material, becoming at once a populariser and an encyclopedist. His work must also be seen as part of the Benedictine response to the political challenges of the rise of new orders. The black monks were called upon to defend their rights as priests in the care of souls. The works of Honorius provide training in catechism and sermonising necessary in pastoral work. The clarity and simplicity of his style may also have contributed to the wide demand for his works. The *Elucidarius*, probably his earliest work, is a school book in dialogue form, in which a student patiently poses and a master answers questions of faith. The *Speculum ecclesiæ* is a collection of sermons arranged in order of the liturgical calendar. The *Imago mundi* summarises the knowledge of the natural sciences, while the Gemma animæ provides meditations on and explanations of liturgy and ecclesiology. And for guidance in the devotion to Mary, there is the *Sigillum*.

THE SIGILLUM

The *Sigillum*, or *Seal of Blessed Mary*, is the second on the list of Honorius' works in *De luminaribus*, after the *Elucidarius*. The brothers thank him for the receipt of it in the prologue to the *Inevitabile*.[19] Honorius also mentions this earlier effort at exegesis of the Canticle in his later commentary, the *Expositio in canticum canticorum*.[20]

Scholars have virtually dismissed the *Sigillum*. If dated into the 1120s, it becomes a mediocre derivative of Rupert of Deutz's more exhaustive Marian reading of the Canticle *ca.* 1125.[21] But Honorius is clearly unaware of Rupert's work and takes a rather different approach, one responsive to devotional and liturgical facets of his subject. Moreover, Flint's revised chronology for Honorius' works forces us to reevaluate this early text. By virtue of its subject and its sources, the *Sigillum* is part of the group of works closely associated with England. If the *Elucidarius* was composed just before 1100, the *Sigillum* would have followed it directly, early in the twelfth century, probably by 1103. The composition date of *ca.* 1100 makes it the first commentary on the Canticle to focus on its application to

Mary.[22]

The *Sigillum* also suffers in comparison to Honorius' second commentary on the Canticle. Honorius himself promoted the later over the earlier effort, and the *Expositio* precedes the *Sigillum* in a majority of the manuscripts. In his second commentary, he provides an entirely different interpretation, developing the ecclesiological and eschatological levels of his text. Perhaps in reaction to the textbookish compilation of the *Sigillum*, Mary figures in this later work only peripherally. Honorius reasons that the *sponsa* of the Canticle is four distinct personæ, allegorical daughters who represent four peoples brought to Christ. The unfolding of the song recapitulates the sacred history of the Church, from Genesis to Apocalypse. Honorius was proud of his achievement, stating in the *De luminaribus* that it "laid out the Canticle of Canticles as no one had ever seen before."[23]

Even Honorius' twelfth-century following held the *Expositio* in higher regard. Honorius' Marian theology was no longer in the vanguard by the late twelfth century when his works were most enthusiastically copied. The *Sigillum* must have seemed terse in comparison to Bernard's rapturous outpourings, superficial when set against Rupert of Deutz' scholasticism, or niggardly in its praise of Mary at a time when her more fervent admirers were proclaiming her Immaculate Conception.[24] In contrast, the more vivid and unusual imagery of the *Expositio* excited the imagination of the Austro-Bavarian cloisters, and it remains the only work of Honorius for which illustrations were devised. The interpretation offered by the mature Honorius is complex, mystical, and even fanciful. Its imaginative freedom is consonant with the individualistic tone of much Biblical exegesis of the second quarter of the century, and in this later text—not the *Sigillum*—Honorius rose to the challenge of Rupert and Bernard.

The *Sigillum* is valuable for being the first of its kind. To be sure, Honorius' explanations are heavily dependent upon earlier sources, but his goal was to accumulate in one place a great deal of material about Mary, often modern and sophisticated, drawn from a variety of sources. He does not strain for an interpretation. As Flint notes of the *Elucidarium* before it, "the really hard work is directed to the end of giving the most reliable answers available; never towards the asking of more questions and the furthering of discovery."[25] But the *Sigillum* is an excellent textbook and in writing it, Honorius was providing not novelty, but authoritative and correct readings of Biblical texts, in response to a pressing devotional need.

THE CANTICLE OF CANTICLES

The fact that, in his maturity, Honorius could turn with such great profit to a text that he had thoroughly researched in his youth is primarily a testimony to the richness and complexity of the Canticle itself.

What does the Canticle *really* mean? Unfortunately there is no simple answer to this question; there is no universally accepted assessment of this poem of love, which has been described as "locks to which the keys have been lost." Its language is possibly the most difficult in the Bible, since the Hebrew is in a dialect form and contains numerous *hapax legomena*, words that occur only once in preserved writing. The language is also rich in metaphor and now-obscure allusions. In the mediæval period this was complicated further by the use of a translation that had passed first into the Greek of the Septuagint and then into the Latin of the Vulgate, rendering many Hebrew words (especially proper nouns) into unclear, if evocative phrases. The poem records a dialogue, but the speakers are not always identified; shifts in person are abrupt and erratic. In fact, scholars now assume that the Canticle is a conglomerate of several once distinct poems.

At its most basic, the Canticle is a song of love celebrating the physical delights of lovers as well as the gamut of emotions connected with being in love. But the Canticle reaches beyond the merely transitory. Elements of the text seem to derive from pagan fertility worship, out of rites in which sexuality is linked to the fertility of the earth and the great seasonal cycles of birth and death. Pope found much comparable material in Semitic, especially Ugaritic, songs recited at the ritual marriage of the goddess Ishtar (as she is known in one of her various incarnations) and Tammuz. Images found in the Canticle are also reflected in Arabic and Syrian cycles of wedding songs. These are old words, then, sung to evoke the ecstacy possible in the union of male and female, and in the union of human and divine.

The inclusion of such a sensual love poem into the Biblical canon has puzzled many. Its spiritual authority comes from Solomon, who figures in the narrative,[26] and, according to the earliest records, is supposed to have composed the text. Solomon's lusts for his foreign wives is well attested, and perhaps this poetry does belong inside the walls of his harem. But Solomon was also possessed of great wisdom and later generations remembered him as an initiate into the secrets of mysticism and magic. Small wonder, then, that the Canticle was probed for its deeper meanings, and its poetic language considered the most proper vehicle for the greatest of mysteries.

Honorius was heir to a long and rich tradition of reading the Canticle as an allegory, and aspects of many traditional interpretations are present in the *Sigillum*. The foundation for all Christian interpretations was Origen's powerful and poetic commentary of the mid–third century which explained the Canticle as a dramatic dialogue between Christ and the believing Soul. Neoplatonist and Gnostic attitudes influenced Origen's transformation of the Canticle into an allegory of spiritual love; the lusty language of the text is not literal, but refers exclusively to inner religious experience. In fact, for Origen, the sensuous poem actually directs the individual toward the denial of the world that is necessary in order to prepare for a union with divinity. Of course, the simple could not be expected to understand this paradox, and thus both Jewish and Christian scholars agreed that the Canticle should only be studied by the most advanced student. Origen admonishes:

> For this reason, I advise and counsel everyone who is not yet rid of the vexations of flesh and blood and has not ceased to feel the passion of his bodily nature, to refrain completely from reading this little book and the things that will be said about it. For they say that with the Hebrews also care is taken to allow no one even to hold this book in his hands, who has not reached a full and ripe age. [27]

With this precedent, in writing on virginity, Ambrose could cite passage after passage from the Canticle in praise of the cloistered life, in order to encourage young women toward contemplation. These ascetic readers of the Canticle had many followers, and this text was perhaps the most beloved among twelfth-century monks, among them, Honorius.

The Jew of late antiquity cherished the Canticle as a record of God's love for his people, a dialogue between God and Israel which traced the progress of the Jews in history. Following that example, Christian commentators turned it into a narrative of Christ and his Church. Concerned with the unification of the Jews and Gentiles, exegetes might specifically see the Canticle as a call to the

Jews to convert to belief in Christ, especially in such a line as "Return, return O Sulamitess" (Cant 6:12). For the high Middle Ages, the authority of Bede stood behind this view, although his work is heavily dependent on the earlier commentaries of Gregory the Great, Cassiodorus, and others. Bede envisioned the Canticle as a dialogue between Christ and the believers, believers both before and after Christ—that is, the Gentiles and Jews—who are the two components of the single Church which is espoused to Christ. Bede thus divides the poem's lines between several characters—Christ, the Church, the Synagogue and their members—and the subject matter of the Canticle is revealed to be the entire history of the faith. The ecclesiological interpretation was adopted in the liturgy, and some texts for the service mark the Canticle into speeches intoned by Christ and the Church, much as Bede and, later, Honorius divide it.

HONORIUS' MARIAN THEOLOGY

Honorius' observations in the *Sigillum* are incontestably part of both the ecclesiological as well as the ascetic and mystical traditions of Canticle commentaries. Honorius' more valid claim to originality is in offering an interpretation of the text based on Mary.

Yet even in this, Honorius was not really breaking new ground. He was responding first of all to the widespread devotion to Mary. Interest in the Mother of God led to the continuous growth of her cult from the early days of the church, the establishment of a number of feasts in her honour and the accumulation of texts—both popular and scholarly, spurious and authoritative—which proclaimed her virtues and powers. Marián devotion was particularly fervent in England. Thus the *Sigillum* must be placed alongside the collections of the *Miracles of the Virgin*, the ecstatic prayers and sermons of Anselm of Bec and his followers, and the extravagant claims of the Immaculists as evidence of the cult of Mary in the British Isles.

Individual passages of the Canticle had already been quoted in one or another Marian context. In the fourth century, Athanasius had suggested that the poem was the Church's song of jubilation at the moment of the Incarnation. Others opined that whereas the Canticle applied generally to the church, it applied specifically *(specialiter)* to Mary. In some respects, Honorius can merely be credited with collecting these isolated references into a single document.

He tells us himself of his method. Following Augustinian tradition, he compares Mary to the Church, and finds them similar in that each is both virgin and mother. Honorius concludes, "Therefore, all that is written of the Church is suitably ascribed to her as well." Now Honorius need only take the standard explanations of the verses of the Canticle and substitute Mary for Ecclesia, and this he seems to have done more than once. For example, all the fathers agree in interpreting Cant 1:6 "lest I begin to wander after the flocks of your companions" as prophesying the influence of heretical sects who insinuate themselves to others as true Christians. In the same vein, Honorius tells us that Cant 1:6 refers specifically to heretics of Marian doctrine, those Gnostics and Docetists who disbelieve in the virgin birth. Similarly the "teeth" which "are as flocks of sheep" (Cant 4:2) were usually interpreted to be the doctors who grind dogma for the rest of the church; for Honorius they were the doctors who expound subtle dogma about the Virgin.

The Canticle was already taken to refer to the glories of virginity. How readily this interpretation could be expanded with special reference to the Virgin Mary. For example, Ambrose read the first verses of Cant 7 to apply to Mary, the "prince's daughter" of noble lineage, born of the House of David, and for him the subsequent phrases are references to the Incarnation. Honorius simply adopts this reading.

The descriptions of the physical charms of the bride could easily be transferred to the most pre–eminent of Christian women. But in Honorius' text, we can never forget that these virtues first belonged to the Church. In Cant 4:5, Mary's breasts represent virtues appropriate to her: the humility and chastity of virgins. But Honorius immediately adds that they represent the active and contemplative life, an image borrowed from Bede's *Mater Ecclesia*. Later, in Cant 7:8, Mary's two breasts "like clusters of the vine" produce the "drink of the Church," that is, the wine of the Eucharist. In these and many such passages, the odours of ecclesiology still linger about Mary. We might even guess that, in the twelfth century, Mary could be considered as much an allegory—a kind of intellectual ideal—as an actual person of flesh and blood.

It is useful to remember that Honorius writes with the specific intention of explaining the readings for the Feast of the Assumption on August 15th. In the first part of the *Sigillum* especially, Honorius relies on earlier treatments of familiar Biblical texts. His exegesis of the gospel reading for the Assumption, the story of Mary and Martha in Luke 10:38–42, is a summary of a homily by Ralph d'Escures, monk and abbot of St. Martin's of Seez.[28] Honorius' discussion of the Epistle (Ecclus 24:11) was adapted from another homily attributed to Anselm.[29] In his Marian reading of the Canticle, Honorius is generally more original, although he is often true to the tenor of earlier exegetes, and is, in some cases, able to follow quite closely the earlier authority of Paschasius, Paul the Deacon, Bede, and Haimo.[30] In order to demonstrate the intercessory powers of Mary, Honorius cites four miracles. Three of these at least are very well known and Honorius might have found them in a number of common sources. Yet it is tempting to associate this recitation with the very early English collections of the miracles by Prior Dominic of Evesham and William of Malmesbury.[31]

Passages from the Canticle had long been drawn into the liturgy for the Assumption. The notion that Mary was taken up into heaven was based on several "eye-witness" accounts, which were treated with suspicion by some scholars and embraced with pious devotion by the masses. The Transitus ascribed to the Pseudo-Melito describes Mary rising in glory as her son calls "Come from Libanus .... (Cant 4:8)." "Draw me after you" (Cant 1:3) she begs her son during her miserable years on earth after his death. Numerous sermons for that feast appropriated even more quotations from the Canticle. The most popular of these is the homily of Paschasius Radbertus, *Cogitis me*, which was quoted extensively in the liturgical office for that day.[32]

Considering the fervour of some of the devotion to Mary, Honorius' work seems almost conservative. First of all, it is short, perhaps stinting in its praise of Mary. Of course, its brevity contributed to its popularity and usefulness. Although Honorius works Mary into every scene of the drama of the Canticle, he certainly does not give her every line of the dialogue. He also retains the figures of the Church (*Ecclesia*) and the Church to be converted of the Jews (a character who is called *Synagoga* in her frequent appearances elsewhere in art and drama) in a manner almost deliberately archaising.

Although the *Sigillum* begins as a dialogue, Honorius quickly abandons that format to take up a style of explication which must have been familiar from oral instruction. Following the text minutely, the teacher glosses or translates each word or phrase. The result is an almost hypnotic prose, whose best effect is captured when read aloud. Honorius' technique subtly changes as he writes. In the early chapters of the Canticle, he seems to apply all phrases to Mary generally, with slim regard for the literal meaning of the text. By the end of chapter two, he has reverted to the more familiar dialogue format, primarily between Christ and Mary. By the end of the Canticle, Honorius has expanded the cast of speakers, marking each voice clearly, into an eschatological drama with Mary as a leading figure.

Honorius denied to Mary much that her more avid devotees were willing to grant. Following his teacher Anselm, Honorius did not believe that Mary was immaculately conceived. Like all humans, she bore the sin of Adam and had to suffer its punishment, death. In the twelfth century, the details of Mary's life and extent of her sanctity were subject to lively debate and honest disagreement. Honorius' was probably the majority opinion; similar scepticism towards the Immaculate Conception was voiced by Rupert of Deutz and Bernard of Clairvaux, much to the amazement and chagrin of later theologians.[33] Honorius found an inspiring model in a Virgin who had to struggle with sin. When he writes of Mary's spiritual exercises in the exegesis of Cant 5:5–8, the results are some of the most personal passages in the *Sigillum*. The text may even be a testimony to Honorius' own moment of spiritual crisis when he made the commitment to the stricter life of the Benedictine monk. Mary's virginity is an important precedent for the vow of celibacy; Honorius claims, in fact, that she is the first person ever to make it.

Honorius uses the poetic language of the Canticle to praise Mary's superior status as the chosen vessel for Christ. Even his title evokes the Incarnation with the metaphor of the *Sigillum* or seal, which Honorius uses again in the *Expositio*:

> An image is carved into a seal, which transmits the image into impressed wax. The seal is the humanity of Christ, and the image carved into it is the divinity of Christ; truly the wax is the human soul, formed in the image of God.[34]

Christ's divinity is impressed on to the wax of humanity. Since his flesh is taken from the Virgin, Mary, herself, is the seal, or the instrument through which Christ appears. She is also wax, the human who has received the finest impression of divinity.

Of course, Mary's purity never comes into question, and her glorification at the Assumption is, in part, a reward for her moral incorruptibility. Honorius intimates that she was without sins of her own commission, and, at the Incarnation, when Mary was overshadowed by the Holy Spirit, she was completely cleansed. Mary has great powers as a mediatrix with her Son. By quoting her miracles and by emphasising her intercession for the Jews at the Last Judgment, Honorius places Mary firmly into the plan of salvation. For Honorius, God's divinity is practically incomprehensible, but it is revealed in images: through Christ's humanity, through Mary, and through the Canticle.

EARLY MANUSCRIPT TRADITION

Honorius' *Sigillum* was a popular text, and is preserved in numerous twelfth–century copies from monastic library collections in England, southern Germany and Austria. These manuscript copies can be divided into three groups. In the first are those manuscripts preserved in England, where Honorius composed the work. The earliest copy of the *Sigillum* seems to be Ms. Jesus College, Oxford, 54 from

Evesham, with the other four English copies preserved from the dioscese of Worcester. The thirteen additional surviving twelfth–century or early thirteenth–century manuscripts are all from German and Austrian monastic libraries.[35] The *Sigillum* is usually found with two of Honorius' other writings: the *Expositio super canticum canticorum*, and the *Hexæmeron*, or *Neocosmos*. In seven of the thirteen, the *Sigillum* is preceded by the *Expositio;* in ten it is followed by the *Neocosmos*, in whole or in part.

It is not obvious why the *Hexæmeron*, or *Neocosmos* should be so frequently copied with the two commentaries on the Canticle. The relationship may be merely circumstantial, that the *Neocosmos* followed the *Sigillum* in an original series of "collected works." There is no internal evidence for dating this writing which was probably written soon after he departed Canterbury. In the *Neocosmos*, Honorius reviews the work of earlier authors—notably Augustine—on the six days of creation, which are interpreted as a parallel to the six ages of the world. It shares with the *Expositio* (and to a certain extent the *Sigillum*) an interest in the outlines of sacred history and its count of the generations preceding Christ relate to questions of Mary's motherhood.

In the *Speculum ecclesiæ* Honorius condensed his own Marian material, even more this time, into a sourcebook for preachers. The *Sigillum* proper closes with the exegesis of the Canticle, but many manuscripts append material from the *Speculum ecclesiæ* concerning the other Marian feasts. These additions appear in all but one of the Austrian manuscripts, in Migne's text, and in the present translation.

The surviving Austro–Bavarian twelfth–century copies of the *Sigillum* are of two types, differing in presentation format and function. The first type, probably earlier, consists of "luxury" editions and includes single treatises and the only illustrated exemplars of Honorius' writing. This type comprises a related group of Austro–Bavarian manuscripts of the *Expositio in canticum canticorum, Sigillum,* and *Neocosmos.* Although they are not manuscripts *de luxe* by the most elevated standards since they are adorned merely with pen and ink drawings or initials, they are all of high quality and constitute the most luxurious copies of Honorius' works. No surviving manuscript can be identified as the prototype of this luxury edition. It is unlikely that any of these manuscripts preserves the original text, for they all omit lines in the transition from Cant. c. 1 to c. 2 for example, and all but one include the addenda from the *Speculum ecclesiæ* concerning other Marian feasts. It has been suggested that the original illustrated exemplar of the Expositio was assembled in Regensburg, perhaps by Honorius himself.[36] This exemplar must also have contained the *Sigillum* and the *Neocosmos,* an arrangement still preserved in six of the twelfth–century manuscripts, including the most elaborately decorated. Some version of the intelligent and beautifully executed cycle of illustrations to the *Expositio in canticum canticorum* is found in five monastic manuscripts of the third quarter of the century: Vienna 942 from Salzburg, the Munich exemplars from Bauerberg, Benediktbeuren and Tegernsee, the Augsburg Universitätsbibliothek I 2 2° 12 from Füssen, and Walters 29 from Lambach. It seems unlikely that the *Sigillum* was ever illustrated but it probably boasted at least three elaborate initials: the "O" of *Optimo magistro;* the "D" of *Dicite,* and the "G" of *Gloriosa regina.*

Any full biography of Honorius must take note of his prominence in the glory days of Regensburg, the second half of the twelfth century. The *Expositio* program is part of a general flowering of symbolic and typological art in the manuscripts of the Regensburg–Prüfening school, the ceiling of St. Emmeram, and such a masterpiece as the Klosterneuburg altar. The *Neocosmos* might be associated with the beautifully-executed pen and ink cycle of the "six days" in the *Hexæmeron* of Ambrose (Munich, Clm. 14399, 1170–75). Honorius is a significant source for the *Speculum virginum* and the *Hortus deliciarum* of southwest Germany. His writings influenced the *Play of Antichrist* (*ca.* 1160) and perhaps other allegorical dramas of the late twelfth century. Honorius' work might also be the inspiration behind the damaged and mystifying sculptural program of the portal of the Jakobskirche itself (late 1180s). The *Speculum ecclesiæ* is much cited in late twelfth–century collections of sermons, while portions of the *Elucidarius* were translated into German in the 1190s.

Of the more elaborate manuscripts, Vienna 942 is the most notable and ranks among the masterworks of the Salzburg scriptorium from the third quarter of the twelfth century. This codex stands out not merely by virtue of the high-quality illustrations, but in its folio size, beautiful script, accurate text and generous layout. The luxuriousness of this copy is exemplified by its wide margins containing identifying rubrics for key concepts in the exegesis of the gospel and Eccelesiasticus texts. (Both Admont 579 and Kremsmünster 114 are plainer copies of a text of this generous format.) Vienna 1023, a late twelfth–early thirteenth century manuscript of unknown provenance, is an excellent copy in folio size, although its decoration is confined to the simplest pen and ink initials. Innsbruck 300, possibly from Wappenbrunn, occupies a unique place in this group, being the least accurate text in the most cramped format, but most richly decorated with gilded initials.

In the second sort of manuscript, the *Sigillum* is collected with works of other authors. These codices, usually comprising fragments selected according to a theme, are less carefully written, and are probably directed toward Benedictines engaged in the secular world as priests and preachers. This functional group attests to the usefulness of Honorius' writing in pastoral training. Kremsmünster 114 is a typical florilegium, containing the enormously popular Miracles of the Virgin, offices for the Marian feasts—complete with neumes—the *Sigillum*, and several sermons on martyrs. This codex, possibly intended for use during the services, is richly decorated with pen and ink initials, some figured, in a lively and exuberant style which reflects the late twelfth-century work of an accomplished artist. Admont 579 is a florilegium collected with an eye toward a student of theology, since the *Sigillum* is copied with other important documents on the Assumption. Vienna 1059 and Wilhering IX. 110 are less-focused collections in which the *Sigillum* is found amidst diverse liturgical tracts, sermons, lives of the saints, and meditational fragments.

It was the Benedictines who first devotedly copied and disseminated the work of Honorius. All these codices are evidence of the profound admiration for the Canticle and the propensity for meditation on sacred history that characterised the twelfth-century cloister, whether ultimately directed toward a life of contemplation or of pastoral activity.

CONCLUSION

Honorius has been diversely assessed by modern scholars. Many have dismissed him as a mere compiler who had nothing new to say. But as the details of his life are revealed, his contribution must be viewed in a more favourable light. His works can be dated much earlier than previously thought, placing Honorius at the origins of developments which others thought he merely reflected. He is among the first to introduce scholasticism into Germany, having assimilated the doctrines of Anselm. He was likewise an early advocate of monastic reform and an important defender of the rights of the Benedictines challenged by new orders and political structures. The *Sigillum* was one of the first extended Marian readings of the Canticle in a century that will be dominated by Marian theology. Even his compulsion to compile must be seen as part of the mission felt by the most progressive schoolmen to organise knowledge into a systematic and consistent whole.

Honorius is certainly not a pedantic writer of dry and rigid textbooks. His aim was both to instruct and delight. The poetic titles of his works are one indication of his sensibilities; two commentaries on the heady text of the Canticle reflect his yearnings for the ineffable rewards of the contemplative life. The *Speculum ecclesiæ* has been recently praised as the most significant instrument for the revival of preaching in the late twelfth and early thirteenth centuries.

Honorius' audiences were stimulated by the concordances he established between the "visible figurations" of nature, scripture and liturgy. By dealing with the world of flesh and spirit in concrete, readily-visualised terms, he significantly shaped the taste for typology and allegory so evident in twelfth-century art and drama. The *Sigillum* promotes the significant events of the life of the Virgin—specifically her Death and Assumption—and thus contributed greatly to the creation of the official iconography of Mary's life. Illustrations of those scenes are found with increasing frequency in the twelfth century, first in England, and then on the continent. After the first sculptural rendition of the Coronation of the Virgin at Senlis, no Gothic cathedral was without its Marian portal.

Since Honorius is faithful to church teachings, we might not notice the impact of his ideas which encourage themes either traditional or soon to become commonplace. But as Flint notes, he "is rich in small, sometimes irritating tricks of invention," so we are always rewarded with numerous insights and unforgettable images. It is no longer possible to dismiss Honorius as an anti–intellectual or a drudge. He must be given credit for timely commentary on the most important issues of twelfth–century intellectual life.

In consolidating so many strains of Marian liturgical exegesis into the evocative, yet manageable text of the *Sigillum*, Honorius made a valuable contribution to the monastic libraries of the twelfth century. In turn, modern readers can find in him a neat summary of the Mariolatry that pervades every aspect of high mediæval imagination.

EDITION

The following text is a translation of the text in Migne's *Patrologia Latina*, v. 172, cols 495-513, amended with reference to seven manuscripts on microfilm in the Hill Monastic Manuscript Library (HMML), of St. John's, in Collegeville, Minnesota, all preserved from Austrian monastic libraries. Although this does not constitute a critical edition of the *Sigillum,* the corrections from the HMML manuscripts give some idea of its "Austrian" recension. Three manuscripts preserved in Munich and the recently re-discovered text in Augsburg must also belong to this group. In their illustrations, at least, they are related to Vienna 942, but I have not been able to study their texts.

Page references to the *Patrologia latina* are included in brackets in the text, as are editorial additions. The passages added and corrections made on the basis of the HMML manuscripts are explained in the notes. Where the Migne text has been changed significantly, the manuscript authority will be cited in the notes, abbreviated as follows: VS=Vienna 942 from Salzburg; Va=Vienna 1023; Vb=Vienna 1059; A=Admont 579; I=Innsbruck Univ. Bibl. 300; K=Kremsmünster 114; and W=Wilhering Cod. IX, 110. Biblical citations are quoted in the Douay-Rheims translation of the Vulgate, except where noted. The complete text of the Canticle is also provided as an aid to the reader.

Thanks to Richard Kieckhefer, the Medieval Latin Workshop at Northwestern University (1986-1987), Barbara Newman, Peg Carr, and the generous support of Julian LaPlante and the excellent staff at the Hill Monastic Manuscript Library, St. John's, Collegeville, Minnesota.

CANTICLE OF CANTICLES

CHAPTER 1

Mary
1 Let him kiss me with the kiss of his mouth: for your breasts are better than wine.
2 Smelling sweet of the best ointments. Your name is as oil poured out: therefore young maidens have loved you.
3 Draw me: we will run after you to the odor of your ointments. the king has brought me into his storerooms: we will be glad and rejoice in you, remembering your breasts more than wine: the righteous love you.
4 I am black but beautiful, O you daughters of Jerusalem, as the tents of Cedar, as the curtains of Solomon.
5 Do not consider me that I am brown, because the sun has altered my color: the sons of my mother have fought against me, they have made me the keeper in the vineyards: my vineyard I have not kept.
6 Show me, O you whom my soul loves, where you feed, where you lie in the midday, lest I begin to wander after the flocks of your companions.

Christ
7 If you know not yourself, O fairest among women, go forth, and follow after the steps of the flock, and feed your kids beside the tents of the shepherds.
8 To my company of horsemen, in Pharao's chariots, have I likened you, O my love.
9 Your cheeks are beautiful as the turtledove's, thy neck as jewels.
10 We will make you chains of gold, inlaid with silver.

Mary

11 While the king was at his repose, my spikenard sent forth the odor thereof.

12 A bundle of myrrh is my beloved to me, he shall lie between my breasts.

13 A cluster of cypress my love is to me, in the vineyards of Engaddi.

Christ

14 Behold you are fair, O my love, behold you are fair, your eyes are as those of doves.

Mary

15 Behold you are fair, my beloved, and comely. Our bed is flourishing.

16 The beams of our houses are of cedar, our rafters of cypress trees.

CHAPTER 2

1 I am the flower of the field, and the lily of the valleys.

Christ

2 As the lily among thorns, so is my love among the daughters.

Mary

3 As the apple tree among the trees of the woods, so is my beloved among the sons. I sat down under his shadow, whom I desired: and his fruit was sweet to my praise.

4 He brought me into the cellar of wine, he set in order charity in me.

5 Stay me up with flowers, compass me about with apples: because I languish with love.

6 His left hand is under my head, and his right hand shall embrace me.

Christ

7 I adjure you, O you daughters of Jerusalem, by the roes, and the harts of the fields, that you stir not up, nor make the beloved to awake, till she please.

Mary

8 The voice of my beloved is like a roe, or a young hart. Behold he stands behind our wall, looking through the windows, looking through the lattices.

10 Behold my beloved speaks to me;

Christ

Arise, make haste, my love, my dove, my beautiful one, and come.

11 For winter is now past, the rain is over and gone.

12 The flowers have appeared in our land, the time of pruning is come: the voice of the turtle is heard in our land:

13 The fig tree has put forth her green figs: the vines in flower yield their sweet smell. Arise, my love, my beautiful one, and come:

14 My dove in the clefts of the rock, in the hollow places of the wall, show me your face, let your voice sound in my ears: for your voice is sweet, and your face comely.

15 Catch us the little foxes that destroy the vines: for our vineyard has flourished.

Mary

16 My beloved to me, and I to him who feeds among the lilies,

17 Till the day break, and the shadows retire. Return: be like, my beloved, to a roe, or to a young hart upon the mountains of Bether.

CHAPTER 3

1 In my bed by night I sought him whom my soul loves: I sought him, and found him not.
2 I will rise, and will go about the city: in the streets and the broad ways I will seek him whom my soul loves: I sought him and I found him not.
3 The watchmen who keep the city, found me: Have you seen him, whom my soul loves?

Angels

4 A little.

Mary

When I had passed by them, I found him whom my soul loves: I held him: and I will not let him go, till I bring him into my mother's house, and into the chamber of her that bore me.

Christ

5 I adjure you, O daughters of Jerusalem, by the roes and the harts of the fields, that you stir not up, nor awake my beloved, till she please.

Angels

6 Who is she that goes up by the desert, as a pillar of smoke of aromatical spices, of myrrh, and frankincense, and of all the powders of the perfumer?

Church

7 Behold threescore valiant ones of the most valiant of Israel, surrounded the bed of Solomon.
8 All holding swords, and most expert in war: every man's sword upon his thigh, because of fears in the night.

Doctors
9 King Solomon has made him a litter of the wood of Libanus
10 The pillars thereof he made of silver, the seat of gold, the going up of purple: the midst he covered with charity for the daughters of Jerusalem.
11 Go you forth, you daughters of Sion, and see king Solomon in the diadem, wherewith his mother crowned him in the day of his espousals, and in the day of the joy of his heart.

CHAPTER 4

Christ
1 How beautiful are you, my love, how beautiful are you! your eyes are doves' eyes, besides what is hid within. Your hair is as flocks of goats, which come up from mount Galaad.
2 Your teeth as flocks of sheep, that are shorn, which come up from the washing, all with twins, and there is none barren among them.
3 Your lips are as a scarlet lace: and your speech sweet. Your cheeks are as a piece of a pomegranate, besides that which lies hid within.
4 Your neck, is as the tower of David, which is built with bulwarks: a thousand bucklers hang upon it, all the armour of valiant men.
5 Your two breasts like two young roes that are twins, which feed among the lilies.
6 Till the day break, and the shadows retire. I will go to the mountain of myrrh, and to the hill of frankincense.
7 You are all fair, O my love, and there is not a spot in you.

8 Come from Libanus, my spouse, come from Libanus, come: you shall be crowned from the top of Amana, from the top of Sanir and Hermon, from the dens of the lions, from the mountains of the leopards.

9 You have wounded my heart, my sister, my spouse, you have wounded my heart with one of your eyes, and with one hair of your neck.

Christ, as Mary arrives at the Father's house

10 How beautiful are your breasts, my sister, my spouse! your breasts are more beautiful than wine, and the sweet smell of your ointments above all aromatical spices.

God the Father

11 Your lips, my spouse, are as a dropping honeycomb, honey and milk are under your tongue; and the smell of your garments, as the smell of frankincense.

Christ

12 My sister, my spouse, is a garden enclosed, a garden enclosed, a fountain sealed up.

13 Your plants are a paradise of pomegranates with the fruits of the orchard. Cypress with spikenard

14 Spikenard and saffron, sweet cane and cinnamon, with all the trees of Libanus, myrrh and aloes with all the chief perfumes.

15 The fountain of gardens: the well of living waters, which run with a strong stream from Libanus.

God the Father

16 Arise, O north wind, and come, O south wind, blow through my garden, and let the aromatical spices thereof flow.

CHAPTER 5

Mary

1 Let my beloved come into his garden, and eat the fruit of his apple trees.

Christ

I am come into my garden O my sister, my spouse. I have gathered my myrrh, with my aromatical spices: I have eaten the honeycomb with my honey, I have drunk my wine with my milk: eat, O friends, and drink, and be inebriated, my dearly beloved.

Mary, to Church

2 I sleep, and my heart watches: the voice of my beloved knocking: Open to me, my sister, my love, my dove, my undefiled: for my head is full of dew, and my locks of the drops of the nights.

3 I have put off my garment, how shall I put it on? I have washed my feet, how shall I defile them?

4 My beloved put his hand through the hole, and my bowels were moved at his touch.

5 I arose up to open to my beloved: my hands dropped with myrrh, and my fingers were full of the choicest myrrh.

6 As I opened the bolt of my door to my beloved: but he had turned aside, and was gone. My soul melted when he spoke: I sought him, and found him not: I called, and he did not answer me.

7 The keepers that go about the city found me: they struck me: and wounded me: the keepers of the walls took away my veil from me.

8 I adjure you, O daughters of Jerusalem, if you find my beloved, that you tell him that I languish with love.

Church

9 What manner of one is your beloved of the beloved, O

Honorius Augustodunensis, *Expositio in Cantica Canticorum*
(Vienna Österreichische National Bibliothek, Codex 942)

you most beautiful among women? what manner of one is your beloved of the beloved, that you have so adjured us?

Mary

10 My beloved is white and ruddy, chosen out of thousands.
11 His head is as the finest gold: his locks as branches of palm trees, black as a raven.
12 His eyes as doves upon brooks of waters, which are washed with milk, and sit beside the plentiful streams.
13 His cheeks are as beds of aromatical spice set by the perfumers. His lips are as lilies dropping choice myrrh.
14 His hands are turned and as of gold, full of hyacinths. His belly as of ivory, set with sapphires.
15 His legs as pillars of marble, that are set upon bases of gold. His form as of Libanus, excellent as the cedars.
16 His throat most sweet, and he is all lovely: such is my beloved, and he is my friend, O you daughters of Jerusalem.

Church

17 Whither is your beloved gone, O you most beautiful among women? whither is your beloved turned aside, and we will seek him with you?

CHAPTER 6

Mary

1 My beloved is gone down into his garden, to the bed of aromatical spices, to feed in the gardens, and to gather lilies.

2 I to my beloved, and my beloved to me, who feeds among the lilies.

Christ

3 You are beautiful, O my love, sweet and comely as Jerusalem: terrible as an army set in array.
4 Turn away your eyes from me, for they have made me flee away. Your hair is as a flock of goats, that appear from Galaad.
5 Your teeth as a flock of sheep, which come up from the washing, all with twins, and there is none barren among them.
6 Your cheeks are as the bark of a pomegranate, beside what is hidden within you.
7 There are threescore queens, and fourscore concubines, and young maidens without number.
8 One is my dove, my perfect one is but one, she is the only one for her mother, the chosen for her that bore her. The daughters saw her, and declared her most blessed: the queens and concubines, and they praised her.

Queens and Concubines

9 Who is she that comes forth as the morning rising, fair as the moon, bright as the sun, terrible as an army set in array?

Christ

10 I went down into the garden of nuts, to see the fruits of the valleys, and to look if the vineyard had flourished, and the pomegranates budded.

Penitent Church of the Jews

11 I knew not: my soul troubled me for the chariots of Aminadab.

Mary

12 Return, return, O Sulamitess: return, return that we may behold you.

CHAPTER 7

Christ

1 What shall you see in the Sulamitess but the companies of camps? How beautiful are your steps in shoes, O prince's daughter! the joints of your thighs are like jewels, that are made by the hand of a skillful workman.

Penitent Church of the Jews

2 Your navel is like a round bowl never wanting cups. Your belly is like a heap of wheat, set about with lilies.
3 Your two breasts are like two young roes that are twins.
4 Your neck as a tower of ivory. Your eyes like the fishpools in Hesebon, which are in the gate of the daughter of the multitude. Your nose is as the tower of Libanus, that looks toward Damascus.
5 Your head is like Carmel: and the hairs of your head as the purple of the king bound in the channels.

Christ

6 How beautiful are you, and how comely, my dearest, in delights.
7 Your stature is like to a palm tree, and your breasts to clusters of grapes.
8 I said: I will go up into the palm tree, and will take hold of the fruit thereof: and your breasts shall be as the clusters of the vine: and your odors like apples.

9 Your throat like the best wine,

Mary

Worthy for my beloved to drink, and for his lips and his teeth to ruminate.

10 I to my beloved, and his turning is towards me.
11 Come, my beloved, let us go forth into the field, let us abide in the villages.
12 Let us get up early to the vineyards, let us see if the vineyard flourish, if the flowers be ready to bring forth fruits, if the pomegranates flourish: there will I give you my breasts.
13 The mandrakes give a smell in our gates. All fruits, the new and the old, my beloved, I have kept for you.

CHAPTER 8

1 Who shall give you to me for my brother, suckling the breasts of my mother, that I may find you without, and kiss you, and now no man may despise me?
2 I will take hold of you, and bring you into my mother's house and into the chamber of her that conceived me: there you shall teach me, and I will give you a cup of spiced wine and new wine of my pomegranates.
3 His left hand under my head, and his right hand shall embrace me.

Christ

4 I adjure you, O daughters of Jerusalem, that you stir not up, nor awake my love till she please.

Converted Church of the Jews

5 Who is this that comes up from the desert, flowing with delights, leaning upon her beloved?

Christ

Under the apple tree I raised you up: there your mother was corrupted, there she was deflowered that bore you.
6 Put me as a seal upon your heart, as a seal upon your arm, for love is strong as death, jealousy as hard as hell, the lamps thereof are lamps of fire and flames.
7 Many waters cannot quench charity, neither can the floods drown it: if a man should give all the substance of his house for love, he shall despise it as nothing.

Mary

8 Our sister is little, and has no breasts. What shall we do to our sister in the day when she is to be spoken to?

Christ

9 If she be a wall: let us build upon it bulwarks of silver: if she be a door, let us join it together with boards of cedar.

Mary

10 I am a wall: and my breasts are as a tower since I am become in his presence as one finding peace.
11 The peaceable one had a vineyard, in that which has people: he let out the same to keepers, every man brings for the fruit thereof a thousand pieces of silver.

Christ

12 My vineyard is before me. A thousand are for you, the peaceable, and two hundred for them that keep the fruit thereof.
13 You that dwell in the gardens, the friends hearken: make me hear your voice.

Mary

14 Flee away, O my beloved, and be like to the roe, and to the young hart upon the mountains of aromatical spices.

SELECT BIBLIOGRAPHY

Bauerreiss, Romuald. "Zur Herkunft des Honorius Augustodunensis" *Studien und Mitteilungen* 53 (1935): 28-36.

— "Honorius von Canterbury (Augustodunensis) und Kuno I, der Raitenbucher, Bischof von Regensburg 1126-1136" *Studien und Mitteilungen* 67 (1946): 306-13.

Endres, Joseph Anton. *Honorius Augustodunensis. Beitrag zur Geschichte des geistigen Lebens im 12. Jahrhundert.* Kempten: Jos. Kosel, 1906.

Flint, Valerie I. J. "Heinricus of Augsburg and Honorius Augustodunensis: Are They The Same Person?" *Revue bénédictine* 92 (1982): 148–58.

— "The Career of Honorius Augustodunensis. Some Fresh Evidence," *Revue bénédictine* 82 (1972): 63-86.

— "The Chronology of the Works of Honorius Augustodunensis" *Revue bénédictine* 82 (1972): 215-42.

— "The Commentaries of Honorius Augustodunensis on the Song of Songs" *Revue bénédictine* 84 (1974): 196-209.

— "The Original Text of the Elucidarium of Honorius Augustodunensis From The Twelfth Century English Manuscripts" *Scriptorium* 17 (1964): 91-94.

— "The Place and Purpose of the Works of Honorius Augustodunensis" *Revue benedictine* 87 (1977): 97-127.

Garrigues, Marie–Odile. "Honorius était–il bénédictin?" *Studia monastica* 18 (1977): 27–46.

— *Honorius Augustodunensis et la Summa gloria* in *Positions des thèses, Ecole Nationale des Chartes* (Paris, 1967): 39-46.

Graef, Hilda. *Mary: A History of Doctrine and Devotion*, v.

1: *From the Beginnings to the Eve of the Reformation.* New York: Sheed and Ward, 1963.

Littledale, Richard Frederick. *A Commentary on the Song of Songs.* London: Joseph Masters & Son, 1869.

Matter, E. Ann. *The Voice of My Beloved: The Song of Songs in Western Medieval Christanity.* Philadelphia: University of Pennsylvania Press, 1990.

Menhardt, Hermann. "Die Mandragora im Millstätter Physiologus, bei Honorius Augustodunensis und im St. Trudperter Hohenliede" in *Festschrift für Ludwig Wolff zum 70. Geburtstag,* ed. Werner Schroder (Neumünster, 1962): 173–194.

—"Der Nachlass des Honorius Augustodunensis" *Zeitschrift für deutsches Altertum und deutsche Literatur* 89 (1958): 30, 51-4.

Migne. *Patrologia Latina.* Honorius' works are collected in v. 172. [Cited as *PL*]

Ohly, Friedrich. *Hohelied–Studien.* Wiesbaden: F. Steiner, 1958.

Pope, Marvin H. *Song of Songs: A New Translation,* with introduction and commentary, The Anchor Bible. Garden City, New York: Doubleday, 1977.

Reynolds, R.E. "Further Evidence for the Irish Origins of Honorius Augustodunensis" *Vivarium* 7 (1969): 1-8.

Sanford, Eva M. "Honorius, Presbyter et Scholasticus" *Speculum* 23 (1948): 397–425.

Southern, R.W. *Saint Anselm and his Biographer.* Cambridge: Cambridge University Press, 1963.

— "The English Origins of the 'Miracles of the Virgin'" *Medieval and Renaissance Studies* 4 (1958): 176–216.

Weber, Robert, and Bonifatius Fischer. *Biblia sacra iuxta Vulgatam versionem.* Stuttgart: Wurttembergische Bibelanstalt, 1975.

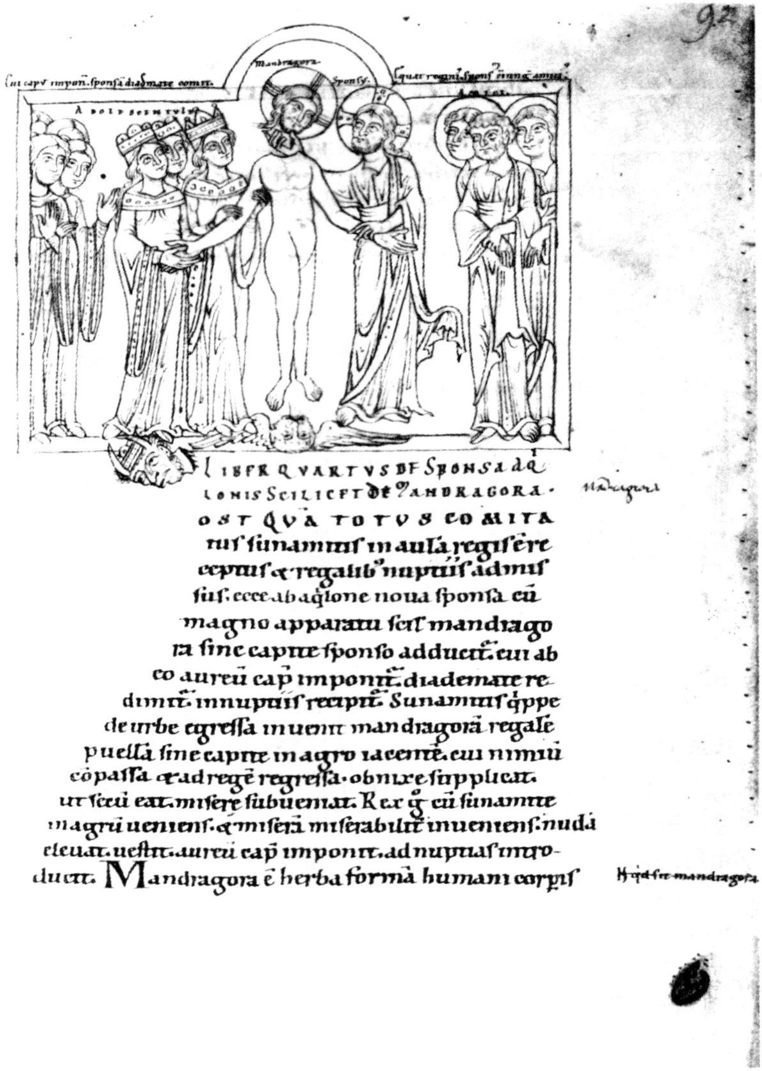
Liber quartus de sponsa aquilonis scilicet de mandragora.
Post quam totus comitatus sunamitis in aula regis est receptus et regalibus nuptiis admissus. ecce ab aquilone noua sponsa cum magno apparatu scilicet mandragora sine capite sponso adducitur. cui ab eo aureum caput imponitur. diademate redimitur. in nuptiis recipitur. Sunamitis quippe de urbe egressa inuenit mandragoram regalem puellam sine capite in agro iacentem. cui nimium compassa et ad regem regressa. obnixe supplicat. ut secum eat. misere subueniat. Rex quoque cum sunamite in agrum ueniens. et miseram miserabiliter inueniens. nudam eleuat. uestit. aureum caput imponit. ad nuptias introducit. Mandragora est herba formam humani corporis

Honorius Augustodunensis, *Expositio in Cantica Canticorum*
(Vienna Österreichische National Bibliothek, Codex 942)

SIGILLUM BEATAE MARIAE
THE SEAL OF BLESSED MARY
WHEREIN IS EXPOUNDED
THE CANTICLE OF CANTICLES

Disciples to the Master:[1]

To the excellent master, with the register of books *[librorum registro]*; from the assembly of students; may you see in Sion the God of Gods.[2] The convent of all the brothers thanks you because the Spirit of Wisdom working through you in the *Elucidarium* lifted so many veils for them. We all beg you, therefore, to undertake a new work and show us, in the spirit of Charity, why the Gospel text *Jesus entered into a certain town* (Lk. 10:38) and the Canticle of Canticles are read on the Feast of Mary, although they do not seem to pertain to her at all.

Response of the Master:

Because I have determined to bear the burden of the day and the heats in the vineyard of the Lord for a mere penny,[3] I do not wish to occupy the earth in vain, like a sterile fig tree,[4] but to provide some adornment for the House of God, like a fruitful olive,[5] so that someday I may deserve to receive a mansion therein.[6] Therefore, because you have so gladly received the little book which I sent, I will endeavour to unlock for you, by the Key of David those matter on which you seem to have doubts. Therefore let this book be brought forth, to the glory of the Son of God and the honour of his mother, and let it be called the Seal of St. Mary. And may he bestow discernment *[intellectum]* whose wisdom surpasses all understanding *[sensum]*.

THE SEAL OF ST. MARY

You say that you wonder why the Gospel text *Jesus entered* and the Canticle are read on the feast of the blessed Mary [the Assumption], although neither of them is seen by simple people to say anything about her. First of all, then, you should know about this Gospel that in all of Scripture [497] there is nothing more fitting, more suitable, more worthy to be read on her sacred feast. The text reads: *Jesus entered into a certain town* (Lk. 10:38). In the town there is a high tower which has ramparts against enemies; and a wall on the outside as a protection for the citizens within. This town was that sanctuary of the Holy Spirit, namely the glorious Mother of God, the Virgin Mary, who was fortified on all sides with the unfailing protection of the angels. In her there is a high tower, that is to say, humility, reaching to the highest heaven, whence it is said: *He has regarded the humility of his handmaid* (Lk. 1:48). The wall outside was her chastity which furnished a defense for the rest of the virtues within. The Lord entered this town when he took human nature to himself in the womb of the Virgin. *And a certain woman named Martha, received him into her house. And she had a sister called Mary.* Martha signifies the active life and Mary the contemplative life, both of which the ever-virgin Mary is said to have cultivated more perfectly in Christ. She provided for him all the works of the Gospel through the ministry of the active life. For into the lodging of her womb, adorned with jewels of virtue, she took him, who from childhood was an exile from his kingdom[7] for our sake, a stranger in this world. With her own breasts she nourished him when he was hungry, she consoled him on her knees when he was weeping. She warmed him with baths when he was ill, she wrapped him up in swaddling clothes when he was naked,[8] she wrapped him with bands when he was crying, she planted sweet kisses on him when he was smiling. She was exceedingly busied with constant service, fleeing from the face of Herod into Egypt, returning again only to find Archelaus in his place. She was *much troubled* about many things, seeking everywhere safe hiding places to conceal him. When Martha is said to complain about her sister leaving her alone in her work, what this means is that Mary, seeing Christ seized by the impious, cruelly dragged off, bound, boxed about the ears, beaten, mocked, condemned with thieves, bitterly crucified on the gallows of the cross, if it had been possible, would freely have given her life for his deliverance. And although she knew that divinity dwelt bodily within him, in a way she was troubled in her mind and complained that divinity did not come to his aid, but deserted him like something noxious, whom it exposed to so many evils, like something cast off. Sitting at the Lord's feet, she longed for his words in her heart and ear, which she who kept these words in her heart pondering them in contemplation as she meditated on spiritual things and longed for heavenly things. The Fount of Wisdom himself had made a dwelling place in her and therefore all the treasures of wisdom and knowledge were hidden in her. Being now released from Martha's labour, the real and not symbolic Mary[9] enjoys in that heavenly life *the one thing necessary.* Enfolded perpetually in her Son's embraces, along with the angels, she is satisfied with the beholding of his divinity. To which glory today the glorious Virgin departed; in which glory her Son[10] exalted her above all the ranks of angels as Queen of Heaven. Today she received twofold from the hand of the Lord *the best part* which she chose while here, *which shall not be taken away from her,* but will be multiplied a hundredfold when the fullness of joy is given to the saints.

CONCERNING THE EPISTLE

As to why the reading concerning[11] praise of Wisdom (Ecclus 24:11–23) is read on her day, [498] there is sufficient reason: Christ is the Wisdom of God, whose personification says in this text: *I sought rest in all these,* meaning these people, but I found a place *to abide* only *in the inheritance of the Lord,* that is, in the Church. And giving thanks, she adds: *He that made me rested in my tabernacle.* The tabernacle of the Church, or of God, is blessed Mary ever virgin, as is said: *He has set his tabernacle in the sun.* In which the Son of God, coming as a man, rested, and from which he proceeds as a bridegroom in the bridal chamber. *Let your dwelling be in Jacob and your inheritance in Isræl and take root in my elect.* Jacob, the uprooter of vices, is the apostolic order; and he is also Isræl, which is to say, a man who sees God. The virgin of God lived in that Jacob, and she inherited the kingdom of God with that Isræl, and into these elect[12] she sent the roots of her own chastity and humility. *And so I was established in Sion.* Sion is called the watchtower and it is the Church, in which the mother of God is established as a column by writing and preaching; and upon her praiseworthy life the whole Church is supported. *And in the holy city likewise I rested.* The holy city is the supernal homeland, illumined by an eternal brightness. In which the perpetual virgin now rests with saints and angels, but crowned with glory and honour, she shines above all the rest. Whence it says: *My power is in Jerusalem.* The present church is called Sion and the heavenly homeland is called Jerusalem. Moreover, Mary is called Queen of Heaven, so her power is not unrightly spoken of as in Jerusalem.[13] And because she *took root in an honourable people* here, that is in a believing people, by the example of her holiness, therefore, her *inheritance* will be *in the portion of her God,* that is, in the divinity of the Son himself. *And* this will be in *the full assembly of saints,* that is, when the number of the elect is complete, she will have praise and glory from all. *I am exalted as a cedar in Libanus.* Libanus is a mountain in the promised land on which there is a cedar[14] from whose roots the river Jordan flows. Libanus means spiritual brightness [candidatio], and is the Jewish people, newly cleansed in the worship of God and holy scripture.[15] In their midst the glorious Virgin was exalted as a cedar, which is to say that she surpassed the merits of all in the odour and beauty of her sanctity; as the Jordan flowed from the mountain, he who consecrated the font of baptism for the world flowed from her womb. *As a cypress tree on Mt. Sion.* A cut cypress does not grow back, thus, of old it was carried at the head of the funeral procession. Thus the virgin Mary, mother of God, was the cypress on Mt. Sion, to wit, on the true watchtower, that is to say, the Church, whose mind, once it has dried up vices and desires,[16] never grows back to the joys of the world; therefore she is held up in preaching as a model before those who are to be mortified for Christ's sake. *I was exalted as a palm tree in Cades.* The palm is given to victors, and that is the meaning of Cades, that is, the sanctified ones to whom the beloved Virgin is the palm of holiness, since through her they gain the abundant offspring of victory and sanctification. *As a roseplant in Jericho.* Jericho means the moon, that is, the Church within which the rose signifies the martyrs, all of whom the holy Theotokos[17] surpasses by the eminence of her own passion, just as the rose excels all other flowers in redness. [499] For when she saw the Son of God born of her so innocently tortured on the cross, she endured in her soul a torment greater by far[18] than that of all the martyrs. Thus she was greater than a martyr, for they suffered in body, but she suffered in spirit, as it is said: *And your own soul a sword shall pierce* (Lk. 2:35). *As a fair olive tree in the plain.* Oil signifies mercy; the plain is unwatered earth, and signifies virgins who are not furrowed by the plowshares of virile embrace. Among these, the pure Christ-bearer is especially fair, like a graceful olive in the plain, whence flowed the oil of joy and mercy which healing us of infirmity, anoints us unto the glory of the kingdom of heaven. *As a plane tree by the waters in the streets was I exalted.* The waters are the people milling through the streets, that is, in the life of the world, or rather, shining forth in the married state; among whom the noble Virgin shone forth as a plane tree, since in her fertility she produced noble offspring. *Like cinnamon.* Cinnamon means the unstained, and signifies the innocents for whom the Virgin was a stick [virga] of cinnamon,[19] since out of her immaculate womb she brought forth the bestower of innocence. It is furthermore an aromatic tree of ashen color and signifies the penitents for whom again this glorious Virgin was cinnamon, since she gave forth the life of Jesus as her remedy for them. *I gave a sweet smell like aromatical balm.* Balsam smells sweet; with it, the foreheads of Christians are marked and priests and temples of God are consecrated. Like a precious balm, this Virgin gave forth an odour when she brought forth into the world Christ, the sweet odour of souls, who marks us with chrism as members of his kingdom and consecrates us as his temples, he who is king and priest consecrates us as kings and priests.[20] *Like the best myrrh.* With myrrh the bodies of the dead are embalmed. For all those who renounce the world and have recourse to Christ, this Virgin Mary, of whom we have spoken and of whom we will speak yet more, was not merely myrrh, but the best myrrh, when she crucified her body to the enticements of the world and afflicted herself through fasting and vigils. She breathed *a sweet odour* when she produced Christ the odour of angels, who as myrrh chosen above all others, in death offered himself for us to God the Father as the odour of sweetness, in order that he make us, deadened to sin, partakers of his divinity.[21] Now aided by her of whom we speak, and likewise supported by your prayer, let us turn our pen to the Canticle, and discuss why this is read for her feast.

CANTICLE OF CANTICLES

The glorious Virgin Mary represents the type of the Church,[22] which exists as virgin and mother, for she is proclaimed as mother because she, fertile through the Holy Spirit, daily brings forth children through baptism. But she is said to be a virgin because, serving inviolate the purity of faith, she is not corrupted by vicious heresy. Thus Mary was mother in giving birth to Christ, and remaining closed even after giving birth, she was virgin. Therefore all that is written of the Church is suitably ascribed to her as well. It is said therefore:

CHAPTER I

Let him kiss me with the kiss of his mouth. Kings and prophets had not deserved to see or to hear him. [500] But the Virgin not only deserved to carry him in her womb,[23] but also after his birth to give him abundant kisses and to receive many kisses from his blessed mouth. *For your breasts are better than wine.* He who nourishes the angels in the bosom of the Father, here on earth sucked the breasts of the virgin Mother. *Smelling sweet of the best ointments,* that is, full of the gifts of the Holy Spirit. However, it would not be frivolous to understand literally that the Virgin often anointed her beloved son with the best ointments. *Your name is as oil poured out.* Oil added to other liquids rises to the top, and also makes well the sick. The name of the

Virgin is Mary, which means star of the sea [*maris stella*]. Those who invoke her aid in time of trial, through her rise above all adversities, like oil. Like the Jewish boy whom she protected from flames in the furnace where his father had cast him because he had taken the body of Christ along with his Christian playmates. Those who, sick with sin, rely on her, through the oil of Christ swiftly attain their health [*salutem*], like Theophilus, who renounced Christ in a written pact and consigned himself into the hands of the devil. Through her he regained his handwritten pact from the devil, and he who was guilty earned forgiveness. Likewise, that Mary embroiled in many vices[24] through her not only received pardon for her crimes, but also shone forth in glorious miracles. Those who sail upon the sea of life use her as a guiding star, imitating her humility and chastity, and come safely by her to the port of life. As is reported of a certain person who every day whenever he passed before the altar of the Virgin, bowed and said a "Hail Mary." On his death bed, when demons gathered about him, certain that they would carry him off to the abyss, the holy Virgin suddenly drew near and he confessed to his chaplain. Thus she snatched from the wicked ones this man who had already despaired, and by her aid he safely avoided the whirlpool of Cocytus.[25] *Therefore young maidens have loved you*, that is, the virgins imitate you. *Draw me after you*, she says to her son, meaning to the exercise of virtue. For Mary did not learn from her son to create the heavens, but to be rooted in humility and meekness, as it is said: *Learn of me, because I am meek, and humble of heart* (Matt 11:29). Thus she has been drawn to heaven after Christ. *We will run to the odour of your ointments*, that is, the faithful, hastening toward joys, imitate this exemplary life. *The king has brought me into his storerooms*, that is, the King of glory took her up into eternal life. *We will be glad and rejoice in you*, that is, the faithful take delight from her intercession. *Remembering your breasts.* Mary's breasts were chastity and humility, and in them the fellowship of the just rejoice. *More than wine,* that is, more than human glory, *the righteous love you,* that is, the angels honour you. *I am black,* that is, born among the poor, *as the tents of Cedar,* that is, as it were, from sinner women.[26] *Beautiful as the curtains of Solomon,* that is, I am the curtain of the true peacemaker who protected the ark, that is, Christ. And, therefore, a daughter[27] of Jerusalem, that is, a sharer of the vision of true peace. *Do not consider that I am brown, because the sun has altered my colour,* that is, although I was born from the humble, nevertheless the Son of justice chose me in my humility to be his mother. Thus *the sons of my mother have fought against me,* that is, the prophet sons of the synagogue prophesied concerning me, or else, the apostles, sons of Grace our mother, fought against me, that is, for me by preaching against the heretics [501] who said that I gave birth not to God, but to a phantom, or that I gave birth by man.[28] They *have made me keeper of the vineyards,* that is, the exemplar of virginity for all the churches. *I have not kept my vineyard,* that is, it was not I, but the Holy Spirit who protected my virginity. *Show me, you whom my soul loves.* The soul of Mary loved Christ, so he revealed to her all the secrets of the Father. *Where you feed, where you lie in the midday.* The most chaste virgin Mary was the midday, shining and burning with the Holy Spirit, in whom Christ has turned away the heat of passion.[29] He laid down in her humility, and was nourished in her chastity. *Lest I begin to wander after the flocks of your companions,* that is, make known to all that you reposed in me, lest heretics tear me to pieces, saying: "If a virgin gave birth, it was to a phantom." Your companions will appear through the sacrament, so I wander through their flocks because I am their psalm in their sects and assemblies. *If you know not yourself, O fairest among women.* Mary did not know the stain of filth, and so she was beautiful, that is, blessed among all women. Having gone forth from feminine frivolity, she progressed from virtue to virtue. *After the steps of the flocks,* that is, through the example of the saints, she fed *the kids,* that is, the carnal men, through holy works, *beside the tents of the shepherds,* that is, according to apostolic doctrine. *To my company of horsemen, in Pharoa's chariots, have I likened you, O my love.* Just as the people of God were freed from Pharoa by the rod of Moses, so the Church was freed from the devil by the rod of Jesse, Mary, and her flower, that is, Christ.[30] *Your cheeks are beautiful.* The cheeks of this virgin are her manners in the active and contemplative life, which are bashful, being ashamed to sin, *as the turtledove's,* lamenting earthly things and sighing for the joys of the heavenly kingdom. *Your neck,* that is, the faith which joins her to God as her head, is *as jewels,* that is, an ornament for the entire Church. *We will make you chains of gold, inlaid with silver,* which is to say, the apostles and their followers who composed writing in your honour concerning all these things, adorned with wisdom and eloquence. *While the king was at his repose,* that is, [while] Christ [was] in the bosom of the Father, *my spikenard sent forth the odour thereof,* that is, through humility he entered into the womb of the virgin. For spikenard signifies humility, the odour signifies the Incarnation of Christ. *He shall abide between my breasts,* that is, he will be carried incarnate in my womb. *A bundle of myrrh is my beloved to me.* This was when he was hanging on the cross in her presence. *A cluster of cypress my love is to me,* that is, she rejoiced in his Resurrection. *In the vineyards of Engaddi,* that is, in the churches of the faithful. [502] *Behold you are fair, O my love.* Mary is called his love[31] because she kept the secrets of the Father. *Behold you are fair,* in her humility before God, *behold you are fair,* in her chastity before men.

Beautiful by her virginity, beautiful by her fertility, beautiful in her virtues, beautiful in her works, she is beautiful here on earth according to the praise of men, beautiful in heaven by the praise of angels. She was proclaimed beautiful in two ways, declared to be without inner or outer stain. *Your eyes,* that is, the intentions of your works, *are as those of doves,* that is, they are sincere and simple. Or else your eyes are examples of your conduct, [502] which abounding in the gifts of the Holy Spirit, guide others like eyes. *Behold you are fair, my beloved, and comely.* Coming from the chaste virgin, Christ is fair; coming from the Father he is comely. *Our bed is flourishing.* Mary was the bed of Christ, in whom he rested as in a bed. It is called "ours" because the Father and the Holy Spirit were always with him. It was flourishing in virtues. *The beams of our houses are of cedar, our rafters of cypress trees.*[32] For she is the house of God, in whom he lived. The principal beams[33] are her virtues: prudence, fortitude, justice and temperance. The rafters are her good works.[34]

CHAPTER II

I am the flower of the field. She herself is the field, which means the unwatered earth, undefiled by man, or humble. Her flower is her son; she is the *lily of the valley,* that is, adorned with humble parents. *As the lily among thorns, so is my love among the daughters,* that is, just as the lily surpasses thistles and nettles in comeliness and sweetness, so Mary surpasses all the churches by the comeliness of chastity and the sweetness of sanctity. *As the apple tree among the trees of the woods,* so amid all the prophets and apostles Christ came to Mary, overshadowing her by the Holy Spirit without any carnal delight.[35] *I sat down under his shadow, of him whom I desired,* that is, I now come to rest before the vision of him, where the sun and moon wonder at his beauty. *And his fruit was sweet to my palate,* that is, his glory was sweet to my soul. For I now perceive that because the *King* of glory *has brought me into the cellar of wine,* that is, into the heavenly Jerusalem, *there he set in order charity in me,* so that he whom I loved earlier as my Son, now I might love as my God. *Stay me up with flowers, compass me about with apples.* By flowers, the innocents, by apples, that is domestic trees, the other saints are understood. Above the innocents this innocent one is raised; among the blessed she, more blessed, is glorified. *With love* she languishes, because she desired to look upon God perpetually. *His left hand is under my head, and his right hand shall embrace me.* That is, heavenly and earthly things magnify her. *I adjure you, O ye daughters of Jerusalem,* that is, by the mystery [*sacramentum*] of my incarnation I constrain you, O ye souls of the faithful, speaking *by the roes and the harts of the field,* that is, through the prophets and the apostles, teachers of the people, that you *stir not up the beloved,* that is, that you refrain from disquieting my mother with some perverse doctrine, *until she please,* that is, just as she please,[36] namely, as the prophets and apostles taught, that the Virgin shall bear God and man. *It is the voice of my beloved,* meaning of my son, which commanded all these things. He it is who leapt from the bosom of the Father into his mother's womb. *Behold he comes leaping upon the mountains, skipping over the hills.* One who leaps goes now upwards, now downwards. Christ came into the Virgin as one who leaps, because in his divinity he surpasses mountains, that is, he surpasses the angels. With his humanity on earth, he surpasses the hills, that is, the apostles. From heaven he leaped into the womb of the Virgin, thence into the world, next into hell, and once again into heaven.

My beloved son *is like a roe,* which distinguishes good grasses from bad, for he chooses the good from the corrupt, *or* like *a young hart,* who rests in the shade, for he rested in the chaste Virgin. *Behold, he stands behind our wall.* The wall is our mortality. Behind this wall Christ stood, when he assumed a mortal body from the Virgin. [503] Under this wall we lie imprisoned, for we have been mortal by nature. Yet he stood, not under, but behind the wall, because he was mortal not by nature but by will. He stood there, moreover, so as to push down the wall, that is, in order to destroy death. *Looking through the windows,* born of the Virgin,[37] he looked into the world, when he became known through the apostles. He looked out also *through the lattices,* because through the writings of the prophets he was made manifest. Likewise the blessed Virgin was the window of heaven, through whom the sun of justice shone into the house of the world.

My beloved, that is her son *speaks to me: Arise* from mortal life, *make haste* toward the immortal life, *my love,* that is, my intimate one *[secretalis], beautiful* in chastity, *and come* into the joys of heaven. For now on account of me the *winter* of your distress *has passed, the rain* of your tribulations *is over,* all sorrow *is* entirely *gone. Flowers,* that is, your rewards, *have appeared in our land,* that is, they shine forth in the land of the living. The *time of pruning* draws near, when all affliction will be taken from you and you will receive your recompense. *The voice of the turtle is heard in our land,* that is, the voice of exultation and joy is perpetually heard in the tabernacles of the just. *The fig tree has put forth her green figs,* for you have been fruitful in good works, on account of which you shall be rewarded. *The vines,* that is, the churches, *flowering* with virtues by your example, *have yielded a sweet smell* of good works, on account of which also you shall be crowned. *Arise* from the misery of temporal life, you who in humility are *my love,* and in your chastity are *my beautiful one, and come* into your eternal rewards, *my dove,* that is, you who innocently trust[38] *in the clefts of the rock,* that is, in my wounds which I have endured for your salvation, *in the hollow places of the wall,* that is, you who believe in the promise of holy Scripture, which says: *God himself will come and will save us* (Is 53:5).[39] And again: *by his bruises we are healed* (Is 53:5). For just as walls secure the vineyard, so holy Scriptures secure the Church.

The Virgin called these things to mind when she saw him pierced by nails. *Show me your face, let your voice sound in my ears.* By face we understand the beauty of his glory, by the sound of his voice we mean the praise of the angels. *For your voice is sweet,* that is, yours is the highest praise sounded by the angels, and your face comely, that is, your glory is eminent. *Catch us the little foxes.* Little foxes are heretics *that destroy the vines,* that is, their poisons infect the churches of the simple people, saying: "If a Virgin gave birth, it was to a phantom." These are caught as in a net when they are confronted with this syllogism: God can do all that he wishes; moreover[40] he wanted to be born of a Virgin; therefore, what the Virgin carried was God and Man. *For our vineyard has flourished,* that is, Mary has borne Christ. *My beloved* son spoke *to me* as I have reported, *and I* give thanks *to him who feeds among the lilies,* that is, he delights in the multitude of the cities, *till the day* of eternity *break, and the shadows* of this worldly life retire.

Prayer of the Virgin for the Converts

O my beloved, whom I bore, you who shunned the impure ones, now return to the penitents, and be like to a roe, now separating the pure from the impure. *Or* else be like *to a young hart,* quickly running [504] and taking up the vows and prayers of those who have been converted from wickedness; and placing them *upon the mountains,* that is, make them the comforters of those who are the mountains of *Bethel,*[41] that is, high in virtue in the house of the Lord, which is the Church. For the Mother of God is Bethel, that is, the house of God, wherein lived the Son of God. The mountains are his prophets, who foretold concerning her. They are also the apostles who preached concerning her. The things that she perceives of Christ, she declares in these words:

CHAPTER III

In my bed, that is, in my contemplative rest, *by night*, that is, in this life, *I sought* to understand[42] the divinity of Christ, *him whom my soul loves. I sought him* in his godliness, *and found him not*, that is, I could not reach to his height. And I said: *I will rise*, by my heart, to heavenly things, and in my mind *will go about the city*, that is, the ranks of angels, *in the streets and broad ways*, that is, through the angels and archangels. *I will seek* Christ *whom my soul loves. I sought him* among the orders of angels, and *found not* any of them to be like him. *The watchmen found me*, that is, the angels, *who keep the city*, that is, the Church. There is no doubt but that the angels frequently had conversation with the holy Virgin. And I asked them: *Have you seen him, whom my soul loves?* That is, tell whether you, at least, understand the divinity of Christ. They answered: *a little.* Although the angels know much of God, in comparison to the fullness of the truth, it seems only a little. For none of the angels understands God as God knows himself. For no one knows the Father but the Son, neither doth anyone know the Son but the Father, and he to whom it shall please the Son to reveal him,[43] which is believed to have been done for his mother.

When I had passed by them, that is, when I surpassed their nature in contemplation, *I found him whom my soul loves*, to excel by far all the understanding of the angels. *I held him* believing him equal to the Father, *and I will not let him go,* loving him, *till I bring him* by word and deed *into the house,* that is, into the Church, *of my mother,* that is, of grace, *and into the chamber of her that bore me,* that is, into the assembly of the Synagogue, which is to say: those things I know of Christ, revealed by the Holy Spirit, I announce to the Jews and the Gentiles.

Christ to the doctors, concerning the Virgin.[44]

I adjure you, O daughters of Jerusalem, that you stir not up, as said above, by teaching anything against her, and this is repeated again here, lest anything frivolous is preached concerning her.

Then follows the praise of the angels when they hasten to meet her as she seeks the kingdom of heaven.

Who, that is, how glorious *is she that goes up* to the palaces of heaven, *by the desert,* that is, deserting the dangerous world? She is the *pillar,* that is, the right measure of *smoke of aromatical spices,* namely, of compassion and diverse virtues, and these spices are *myrrh,* that is, the martyrs, *and frankincense,* that is, the confessors, *and all the powders of the perfumer,* that is, all the faithful of Christ. For he is the true perfumer, that is, the physician of souls. The assembly of the just is his collection of herbs. The Virgin was a seasoning of virtues for all of those, like a precious aromatic powder.

What follows seem [505] to be the Church's words on the Assumption of the body of Mary.[45]

Behold threescore valiant ones surrounded the bed of Solomon;[46] the body of the blessed Virgin is the bed of the true peacemaker, namely of Christ. The reference to the threescore valiant ones means that many thousands *of the most valiant of Israel,* that is, of the highest angels who truly see God, surrounded her and led her into heaven. *All holding swords,* that is, defenses against demons, *and most expert in war,* namely, most powerful against airy powers. *Every man's sword,* that is, protection, *upon his thigh,* that is, around the body whose thigh gave birth to Christ, *because of fears in the night,* that is, lest the demons strike fears into them.

*Then follow the words of the doctors
who are teaching concerning her.*

King Solomon has made him a litter. Christ the true king of peace made him a litter, that is, a bed for a feast, *of the wood of Libanus.* That is, he chose the Virgin from among patriarchs and kings, in whom he reclined as in a bed placed for a feast, because the faithful feast on flesh, which he took from the Virgin. *The pillars thereof he made of silver.* The columns by which the life of the Virgin is upheld are the Gospels written of her, which are in truth of silver, meaning that they shine forth and resound with preaching. *The seat of gold.* This was the body of the Lord taken from her, upon which divinity reclined. This was of gold, meaning adorned with wisdom and charity. For the Virgin herself was the seat, in whose womb Christ reclined; it was of gold because it shone with the splendor of chastity. *The going up of purple.* This was the holy cross, on which, by his suffering, her Son made a going up for us to heaven. *The midst he covered with charity,* that is, he filled his public life with the sweetness of charity *for the daughters of Jerusalem,* that is, for the imitation of the faithful. Therefore, *ye daughters of Sion,* that is, the souls which are daughters of the church, *go forth* from your carnal deeds *and see* with the eyes of the heart *king Solomon,* that is, Christ, the true peacemaker, *in the diadem wherewith his mother crowned him,* that is, by the mortal flesh with which his mother Mary enclosed him *in the day of his espousals,* namely on the day of the Nativity, when he espoused the Church, or in the day of Passion, when he gave his soul for her, and *in the day of the joy of his heart*, that is, on the day of his Resurrection, when this very Virgin and the apostles rejoiced as greatly as earlier they sorrowed about his death.

CHAPTER IV
Then follows[47] the Son's Praise of the Mother.

O my love, to whom I confided the secrets of the Father, *how beautiful are you* in humility and chastity! *How beautiful are you* in faith and labouring, and therefore adorned in heavenly glory! Your eyes are simple[48] *like dove's eyes*, who, beholding other birds, do not wish to tear them to pieces. Thus you, seeing young men, did not desire to join yourself with them in impure embraces. *Besides what is hid within*, namely charity. The eyes of the Virgin are the prophets, who long ago foreseeing her, prophesied much about her. Her eyes are the apostles, who made known to the people her glories and the miracles of her son. The apostles were the eyes of doves, because full of the Holy Spirit, they lived simply. [506] Also this blessed Virgin is herself the eye of the dove, because she precedes the church as its leader. Beside which, hid within is that sweet disposition which is seen by God alone. Your hair was not tangled, that through it the souls of young men might be allured. The Virgin's hairs are like modest people, because they cling to her piety like hairs to the head. They are *as flocks of goats, who ascend* to the heights. Accordingly, these ascend from virtue to virtue *into Galaad,* namely to Christ, the mountain of our testament.[49] *Your teeth* were not greedy for dainty food. Those people are the teeth of the Virgin who spoke out, expounding subtle things about her. They are as *flocks of sheep that are shorn, which come up from the washing*, because they have been washed in baptism, and have stripped themselves of worldly things for Christ's sake. *All with twins*, that is, full of a double love, *and there is none barren among them*, that is, none is devoid of good works. *Your lips* were not deceitful, but held back from vanity by the mortification of the flesh, *as* hair held back with *scarlet lace. And your speech sweet*, because it is all about God and the rest to come. They, too, are lips of the Virgin, who made known to others the secrets of God concerning her. Her *speech* is their preaching. *Your cheeks* were bashful before men, avoiding their companionship, besides the shame which is hidden within her heart. *As a piece of a pomegranate* is red outside and white within, thus you grew red in your suffering but white in your chastity. Also her cheeks are virgins, which blush to commit sin. *Your neck* was not outstretched in pride, therefore David, that is to say, Christ, made you a tower, that is to say, a defense for the church. Also the neck of the virgin are those who wrote of her; just as a neck swallows food, they swallowed the word of God, and transmit it to others as if into a body. They are as *the tower of David* impregnable against heretics, *which is built with bulwarks*, that is, instructed with much teachings. *A thousand bucklers hang up on it* for defense of the holy Scripture, *all the armour of valiant men*, for overcoming the wickedness of the heretics who attack the holy Virgin. *Your breasts* have not been touched by the hand of such men. Thus the roe that feeds among the lilies, that is, Christ, who delights in the chaste ones, suckled from her. Also the two breasts of the Virgin are the two laws which are written as proclamations about her and her son. The *two young roes that are twins* are the two peoples of the church, eagerly[50] suckling from the Holy Scripture the milk of teachings about St. Mary. These are they *which feed among the lilies*, that is, they delight in the Scriptures, *till the day break*, that is, Christ, by whose light they behold the glory of the mother of God, *and the shadows retire,* that is, those things pass away which they regard now in a dark manner.[51]

By the following words Christ calls his mother toward heavenly things.

I will go to the mountain of myrrh, and to the hill of frankincense. Which is to say: I will come with the multitude of angels to call forth the queen of the heaven, who is the mountain of myrrh, that is, the exaltation of the martyrs who are myrrh, namely, bitter in the height of suffering,[52] and she is a hill of incense, that is, the exaltation of the confessors, who are incense, because they are a sacrifice to God on high.[53] And I will say these words to her: *O my love,* who bore the secrets of the Father, *you are all fair,* because in your several senses, as I said, you are gracious in virtue. And because *there is not a spot* of sin *in you, come from Libanus,* that is, [507] ascend from the whiteness of chastity to the joys of heaven. *My spouse,* because I am one with the Father, to whom you, remaining closed, bore the Son. *Come from Libanus,* namely, from the beauty of the blessed life, greatly exalted in the chamber of the citizens of heaven. *Come* to spiritual[54] joys, *you shall be crowned from the top of Amana,*[55] that is, you will receive the crown of triumph, which you have won away from the devil, who is mount Amana, who is the bird of night, that is, *he is a king over all the children of pride* (Job 41:25), leading the errants into the night of death. *You shalt be crowned* also, that is, you will receive the crown *from the top of Sanir and Hermon,*[56] that is to say, because the princes of the world are humbled by the fruit of your womb, who themselves were *the dens of lions,* that is, the dwelling of demons, and *the mountains of the leopards,* that is, the fortresses of the heretics. *You have wounded my heart,* that is, for love of you I underwent the torment of wounding on the cross. You are *my sister,* because you are my coheir in the Father's kingdom, and you are a *spouse* because you bore me for God the Father. You have wounded my heart, that is, I was touched within with sorrow when I, hanging on the cross, beheld you sorrowing. *With one of your eyes,* that is, with one maternal affect of your eyes, that is, of good examples, *and with one hair of your neck,* that is, with a single ornament of humility by which you clung to me, as hairs on the neck.

Here follows the praise of the Son rendered to the Mother as she arrives at the house of his father.

How beautiful are your breasts, namely humility and chastity, from which the sobriety of virgins has sucked the milk of sanctity. And therefore, *my sister,* that is, my coheir in the kingdom, and *my spouse,* because you have given birth to virgins for me through your example, *your breasts are more beautiful than wine.* The breasts of the Virgin were examples in active and contemplative life, with which, as if with milk, she nourished the little ones in faith. They were better than wine, that is, more worthy than the teachings of the Law. *And the sweet smell of your garments*[57] *above all aromatical spices,* that is, the sweetness of your works[58] is more acceptable than the observance of carnal sacrifices.

The praise of the Father concerning the Virgin.

Your lips, my spouse, are as a dropping honeycomb. He calls her a spouse because she bore the Son to him. Her lips are those who make known the secrets of God concerning her, and who drop honey like a honeycomb, because all speech concerning her overflows with sweetness. *Honey and milk are under your tongue.* Those who proclaim the Virgin are said to be her tongue. Milk and honey flows from them because their teaching nourishes the wise and the foolish. *And the smell of your garments is as the smell of frankincense.*

The smell of garments are those converted by the renown of her examples, who are frankincense for God, that is, their prayer goes forth from them like incense.

Again Christ concerning his Mother.

My sister, my spouse, is a garden enclosed. She was a garden of herbs and trees, that is, she was full of virtues; she remained closed in giving birth, sealed with the Holy Spirit. *A garden enclosed* because after birth, the seal[59] of her virginity was not opened. *A fountain sealed up.* She was also a fountain, that is, the foremost example of virginity. This fountain was sealed, that is, consecrated by the passion of Christ. [508] *Your plants,* that is, your imitators *are* like *a paradise* of diverse trees. Some of them are *pomegranates,* representing martyrs; some of them are *fruits of the orchard,* that is to say, confessors; some are cypress, who, like ointments,[60] heal others by their examples; some are *spikenard,* that is, the lowly ones. Others are as *saffron,* glowing ruddy with charity; others are *sweet cane,* mortifying vices; others are *cinnamon,* the penitent, and *all the trees of Libanus,* that is, all the faithful to Christ.[61] From you flows *the fountain of gardens,* that is, through you comes the baptism of the faithful. And *the well of living waters,* that is, Christ, who is the wisdom of holy Scriptures. And these *ran with a strong stream from Libanus,* because they flowed forth with the abundance of the Holy Spirit from the splendour of your sanctity.

All this came about because God the Father commanded such things, saying: *Arise, O north wind; and come, O south wind, blow through my garden.* That is, let not the north wind, that is, the devil, have a place for tempting you; but let the south wind, that is, Holy Spirit, possess you as my garden. *And let the aromatical spices thereof flow,* that is, through you let my only son be made flesh.

CHAPTER IV

There follow the words of the Virgin, who desires to meet with Christ.[62]

Let my beloved come, that is, Christ, *into me his garden and eat the fruit of his apple trees,* that is, may he embody in himself the obedience of my works.

The words of Christ honouring his mother.

O my sister, coheir in the glory of the Father, *spouse* of the Father, he to whom you bore me. *I am come* into you *my garden* assuming flesh. *I have gathered my myrrh,* inspiring martyrs through my passion, *with aromatic spices,* that is, with the confessors. *I have eaten the honeycomb with my honey.* By honeycomb is understood the body, by honey is understood the soul of Christ. He ate the honeycomb with the honey when, rising again, the body taken from the Virgin joined above with the soul, never again to die. *I have drunk my wine with my milk.* Milk signifies men, wine signifies angels. He drank wine with milk when, arising in human flesh born by the Virgin, he brought men into the company of angels. Turning at once to the angels, he announced to them gladly: *Eat, O friends, and drink and be inebriated, my dearly beloved.* Which is to say: as revelers are delighted by various dishes and rejoice in the company of friends, so also you angels, my friends, make merry, and rejoice, because I have increased your joys by bringing you a multitude of men. Moreover, I have instituted a new feast when I brought my mother, your queen, into your joys.

*Through the words which follow,
the Virgin consoles the Church
which hitherto has been labouring here below.*

I sleep, that is, I rest in glory, *and my heart watches,* while praying for you. It is *the voice of my beloved,* namely, my Son, who is *knocking,* giving me this counsel: *Open to me,* that is, obtain from me by prayers, that[63] I might have pity on all.[64] *my sister* already in the glory of God: *my love,* bearing divine secrets; *my dove,* full of the Holy Spirit; *my undefiled,* kept from all stain of sin. *For my head is full of dew,* that is, those who believe in the Father are full of errors,[65] and *my locks,* that is, the elect are mingled with the damned. Just as *drops* fallen on the head slide off, so, too, will the reprobate [509] who come to the faith working evil be drawn away *by night,* that is, by the devil.

Then the Virgin speaks.

If you wish my prayers not to be in vain, in these things you should imitate me. *I have put off my garment,* that is, I have rejected worldly things, and I have said: *How shall I put it on?* that is, never will I return to them. *I have washed my feet,* that is, I have walled off my affection, and I said *how shall I defile them?* that is, I will not return to my vomit by pondering worldly enticements.[66] Therefore, *my beloved,* namely God, whom I chose above all others, *put his hand,* that is, his son into the world, *through the keyhole,* namely through me, who became a hole through which he came unto men, narrow by humility, but shining in chastity, and therefore accessible to him alone. *And my bowels were moved at his touch,*[67] that is, they trembled at his entrance. *I arose,* that is, I raised my mind heavenward, *to open to my beloved* by my prayers, so as to appease him for the sake of men and I joined these[68] works to my prayer. *My hands dropped with myrrh,* that is, my exercises of carnal mortification abounded. *And my fingers were full of the choicest myrrh,* that is, my pursuits of various austerities were approved. In this way *I opened to my beloved,* namely to my son, *the bolt of my door.* (In this, the meaning comes to me by intransitive grammar.)[69] For the sacred Virgin was a door, through which Christ entered into the world; and the bolt was the mass of human sins, which is said to be her bolt, because even she is thought to be born in sin. She removed it from the door when she renounced sin with holy living. Or else, an entrance was opened[70] with the beloved, since through her, mercy herself[71] comes into the Church. Whence there follows: *but he had turned aside* through me and passed over into the Church. The Church daily removes the bolt of sin by prayers; through it, an entry unto the grace of Christ opens up to us. *My soul melted* in compunction *when he spoke* of the wondrous and alluring vision of the Father. *I sought him* by thinking about him, and I did not find[72] his greatness, clouded by weight of the flesh. *I called,* greatly desiring him,[73] *and he did not answer me,* demonstrating the majesty of his divinity. *The keepers found me* as I was seeking him in contemplation. They are the angels *who go about the city,* that is, they defend the Church of God. *They struck me* with sorrow when they said that not even they could know God fully, *and wounded me* because they incited me to greater zeal in my quest. *The keepers of the walls,* that is, prophets and apostles and preparers of books, *took away my veil from me,* that is, they taught me to avoid the carnal life. *O daughters of Jerusalem,* rather, faithful souls, for whom I earnestly utter prayers, *I adjure you* by my example, *if you find my beloved* Son, equal of the Father, in contemplation, *that you tell him,* that is, that you signify to him by your good works, *that* just as *I languish with love* for him, so you, too, endure all injuries out of love for him.

Here follows the Church's praise of Christ addressed to the Virgin.

What manner of one is your beloved of the beloved,[74] that is, how splendid is your son begotten of the Father's womb, *O you most beautiful among women*, that is, blessed among all those [510] who give birth? *What manner of one is your beloved of the beloved*, that is, how glorious is your son who comes from the bosom of the Father? Therefore we seek him by faith and deeds *that you have so adjured us*, that is, you have thus[75] taught us by word and example.

Praise of the Virgin for the Son.

My beloved Son *is white*, that is, born of a Virgin, *ruddy* through suffering, *chosen* by the Father *out of thousands*, namely, before the angels and all the holy.[76] *His head is as the finest gold*, that is, just as gold excels all metals, so his divinity excels all things. Or, Christ is the head of the Church and he adorns her with his splendor like gold. *His locks are as branches of palm trees*, meaning crowned with thorns for our victory, *black as a raven*, that is, judged among the wicked. For the locks of Christ are those who cling to him as to a head, blossoming in virtues, like palms, and black, like the crow, blackened by tribulations following the example of Christ. *His eyes are as doves*, shining with the fulness of the Holy Spirit. By the dove, the sevenfold grace of the Holy Spirit is understood, which is said to flourish in seven ways, whence he appeared above the Lord in a dove.[77] And the eyes of Christ are the doctors of the Church, full of the gifts of the Holy Spirit, and they are found *upon brooks of waters*, that is, in knowledge of Scripture. *Which are washed with milk*, that is, whose souls are cleansed by the whiteness of virtues, and *sit beside the plentiful streams*, that is, they live by the most abundant gifts of the Holy Spirit. *His cheeks are as beds of aromatical spices,* because he was lovely to the eyes of all who behold him. His cheeks are modest; they are like beds of aromatical spices, because virtues are gathered there. They are *set by perfumers,* that is, adorned by the teachings of the apostles. *His lips* are fine speeches; they are delightful as lilies, shining forth with the comeliness of chastity, *dropping choice myrrh,* that is, teaching mortification through charity. His lips are those who disclose his will, who drop choice myrrh because they preach the finest works of charity. *His hands are turned and as of gold,* that is, his works are rounded off in perfection, and shining with every grace. *They are full of hyacinths,* that is, with virtues. For his hands are those who do good things, which are turned and of gold, that is, perfected in their manners and remarkable in goodness. They are full of hyacinths, that is, alms–giving. *His belly is of ivory,* that is, the fragility of his humanity is chaste, because he was born of a virgin, and it is like ivory because ivory comes from the elephant, which is said to be the most chaste animal. It is *set with sapphires,* that is, decorated with celestial signs. The belly of Christ is those in the church who are infirm; they are of ivory, that is chaste, set with sapphires, that is, adorned with pure conscience. *His legs* are as *pillars of marble,* that is, his strength shows forth wondrously in Resurrection, which is the unbreakable support of the Church, *that are set upon bases of gold,* that is, upon faith and charity. These legs of his are strong in justice, sustaining others through their example, which are pillars of marble, that is, upright and unyielding to sins, [511] set upon bases of gold, that is, firm in evangelic and apostolic doctrine. *His form is as of Libanus,* that is, he is to the beauty of all the saints as Libanus is the ornament of all mountains. And *as the cedars* before all other woods, so he is *excellent* before all the holy angels. *His throat,* that is, his doctrine or his promise, *is most sweet, and all of him is lovely,* both in humanity and divinity, so that even the sublime contemplation of the angels is not satiated in the vision of him. *Such, as I have said, is my beloved* Son, and *he is now* in the glory of the father *my friend, O ye daughters of Jerusalem,* or of the church of the faithful.

The Church to the Virgin.

Whither is your beloved gone, all of whom is everywhere, *O you most beautiful of women,* that is, most holy of those who give birth? *Whither is your beloved turned aside,* whom no place can hold?[78] Tell us if he comes unto any more intimately, and imitating you in faith and works, *we will seek him with you.*

CHAPTER VI

Here follows the response of the Virgin.

My beloved, whom along with the Father the whole world cannot contain, assuming flesh from me, has gone down from the bosom of the Father *into his garden,* that is, into the Church, to the spice beds where virtues are gathered,[79] *to feed in the gardens,* that is, to take delight in those who are productive, *and to gather lilies,* that is, the chaste ones into the eternal storehouses. I was pleasing *to my beloved* for this purpose, *and my beloved* is pleasing *to me* above all things. *Who feeds among the lilies,* that is, who delights among the ranks of the chaste, and thus tenderly has spoken to me:

[Christ.]

You are beautiful in chastity, and therefore, *O my love,* sweet through pious example, and therefore comely in heavenly glory *as Jerusalem,* that is, as the angels who see the face of the Father and enjoy the peace of the Lord, *terrible* against vices *as an army set in array* against heretics and demons. *Turn away your eyes from me, for they have made me flee away,* which is to say: Take delight in my humanity, because you will not be able to approach perfectly to divinity. For however subtly you examine it with the eyes of the mind, you will only find that it exceeds your capacity. *Your hair* was not *twisted* with gold, therefore it is crowned with the diadem of angels. Her locks also are virgins attaching themselves to her through imitation, who are *as a flock of goats* because they ascend[80] to the summit of virtues, *that appear from Galaad*, that is, they do this to bear witness to Christ. *Your teeth* were not accustomed to greed, therefore now they delight in the sweetness of God. Her teeth also are those who expound subtle things about her, who are *as flocks of sheep* shorn of sin, as those *which come up from the washing* of baptism. *All with twins*, that is, full of twofold delight, *and there is none barren among them*, that is, there are none without good works. *As the rind*[81] *of a pomegranate* glows red, thus *your cheeks*, that is, your modesty, shines outwardly in chastity *beside what is hidden within you*, namely, besides charity which lies within. *There are threescore queens*, that is, many souls who govern their conduct[82] in the active life according to the six works of mercy,[83] and *fourscore concubines*, that is many in the contemplative life strive for the embrace of the bridegroom [512] so that they will be able to arrive at the eight beatitudes,[84] *and young maidens without number*, that is, the faithful people abiding under them. You, though only *one*, surpassed the merits of all, and therefore you alone are chosen before all. *My dove*, into whom I poured out the gifts of the Holy Spirit, *my perfect one*, whom I perfected by gifts of virtues. *She is the only one* held up as an example *for her mother*, namely, the living Church,[85] *the chosen* one *for her that bore her.*[86] The *daughters* of Sion, that is, of the Church, *saw her* with the eyes of the heart, *and declared her most blessed*, as it is said: all generations shall call me blessed (Lk. 1:48). *And the queens and concubines,* that is, the active and contemplative ones, *praised her,* saying thus:

[Queens and Concubines.]

Who is she, that is, of what kind is she, who *comes forth* from the sinful masses, as out of the darkness, *the morning rising,* from whom comes forth the sun of justice to illuminate those who sit in the darkness and shadow of death? She is now *fair, as the moon* in the night, *bright* in the supernal homeland *as the sun* is select among stars, *terrible* in her display of opposition to vices, *as an army set in array* against demons.

[Christ.]

The Virgin has said that the beloved has descended into the garden, and the Son affirms: *I went down* from the bosom of the Father *into the garden of nuts,* by taking on fleshly matter. The nuts are the faithful, outwardly bitter through affliction of the flesh, but sweet inwardly, in their souls. The Virgin giving birth[87] brought forth a fruitful garden in which Christ planted the tree of life, which bore the fruit of eternity for us[88] in his time. Therefore I did this *to see the fruits of the valleys,* that is, to reward the works of the humble, of those living by your example. *And to look if the vineyard had flourished,* that I might make the vines, which are the churches, examine your life, and flourish in good acts by your example; *and if the pomegrantes had budded,* that is, whether,[89] by the example of your patience, they desire to undergo suffering on my behalf.

Here follow the words of the penitent Church, which is to be converted from the Jews.

It laments that it has wandered so long from the Virgin and her offspring, and makes up for its error with these words. *I knew not*, O glorious Virgin, that *you* were full of grace and that a fount of grace flowed out of you. *My soul troubled me*, that is, the zeal for the law which I had within my soul prevented me from knowing,[90] and this comes to pass *for the chariots of Aminadab*, that is, for the gospels of Christ, so that having been repelled by me, they should rather be propelled through the regions of the world.

Exhortation of the Virgin.[91]

O Sulamite, already so long captive to the devil, *return* through faith to the mysteries of Christ. *Return* through hope, *return* through the love of God and neighbor, *return* through works, *that* they who are already in Christ *may behold you*, imitating your words and deeds.[92]

CHAPTER VII

Christ to his mother concerning the Church which is to be converted.

What shall you see in the Sulamitess but the companies of camps? Which is to say: In the Church which is to be converted from the Jews, nothing will be seen except companies of those praising God, and camps of those fighting against vices.

Praise of the converting Church concerning the Virgin.

How beautiful are your steps in your shoes, [513] *O prince's daughter!* The prince is understood to be King David, who is read to have been prince of the people of God. Because the virgin was propagated from his seed, she is called his daughter. Her steps are her affections, which were beautiful in shoes, that is, in saintly examples. *The joints of your thighs are like jewels,* that is to say, your thighs are fortunate from which comes forth the precious pearl, namely, Christ the jewel beyond price, who is the garden of all creation. *That are made by the hand of a skillful workman.* The workman is God the Father, his hand is the Son, through whom he made all things, through whom also the incarnation was brought about. *Your navel,* meaning blessed be your navel, on which hung the Son of God. As a shield hangs from a nail,[93] so the little baby hangs from her breasts.[94] This Son is like *a round bowl never wanting cups,* that is, he offers to all those who thirst for him generous cups of deepest delight. *[Your belly is like a heap of wheat.]* Blessed is your womb, in which lay the only begotten Son of God incarnate, who was the wheat from which is made the bread of the faithful. It is a heap because in it is gathered a believing people, *set about with lilies,* that is, thronging with choirs of virgins. *Your two breasts* are understood as blessed because the wisdom of God sucked from them. They are *like two young fawns that are twins of a roe.*[95] The roe is the Church. The two fawns are two faithful peoples, those of the circumcised and those with foreskin, who, imitating him, sucked the milk of humility and chastity from the breasts of the blessed Virgin. *Your neck* is blessed, because often the arms[96] of the Son of God embraced it. And it is *as a tower of ivory,* because it was firmly fortified against pride with chastity. Blessed are *your eyes,* which saw what kings and prophets were not worthy to see. Or, the eyes of the Virgin are the words of her teaching, which are *like the fishpools in Hesebon,* that is, they are enticements to the ways of penitence, so that she herself said: *And his mercy is from generation unto generations, to them that fear him* (Lk. 1:50), namely, the penitents. *And these are in the gate of the daughter of the multitude.*[97] The gate is the eternal Virgin, through which, although closed, the king of heaven entered into the world unto us. And she is the daughter of the multitude because a multitude of faithful will enter through her into the palace of heaven. Blessed is *your nose* which was privileged to discern in Christ the fragrance of the eternal life. Or, her nose was her foreknowledge, because through the Spirit she sensed the words of the prophets which were to be fulfilled in her. It is as *the tower of Libanus,* that is, it was the protection of Christ, *which looks toward Damascus,* that is, erected against the devil. Blessed is *your head,* which you so often bent to kiss the Son of God, *like Carmel,* that is, encompassed in virtues. Blessed are *the hairs of your head,* which the infant Christ took delight in fondling in his divine hands. And these are *as the purple of the king,* because you tore them in sorrow at the time of his Passion. And they are all *bound in the channels,* that is, fastened in the hearts of believers. When Christ praised his mother, he began with her head, but the Church's praise began with her feet. This is because Christ came from the height to the depths in order to raise his mother to heaven, but the Church ascends from the depths[98] to the heights through the Virgin's merits.

Then follows the praise of the Son.

O mother, *my dearest, how beautiful you are* in chastity, *and therefore comely,* in heavenly glory! And because [514] you are dearest to me of all, therefore you will enjoy heavenly delight. *Your stature is like to a palm tree.* Christ on the cross was a palm tree because through him is obtained the palm of victory. Mary's stature, that is, her high glory, is like to his, because as he is the king of heaven, so, too, is she the queen of the angels. *And your breasts like to clusters of grapes,* that is, your merits are like those of the martyrs who are pressed in suffering like clusters of grapes. And it was thus it happened, because *I* myself *said,* that is, I determined it with the Father: I will assume flesh from a Virgin. I will go *up into the palm tree,* that is, into the cross, *and will take hold of the fruit thereof;* I will draw all things to myself. And then *your breasts shall be as the clusters of the vine,* that is, your merits shall be imitable by all, like my gospels, which are clusters of the vine, namely, the drink of the Church. And this is the cluster which the sons of Isræl carried upon a lever.[99] The lever was the cross and the cluster was Christ; those who carried it were the apostles and prophets. The vine which bore the cluster was the blossoming body of the Virgin. The cluster of grapes was pressed in the winepress of the cross, and out of it flowed the drink of the faithful.[100]

And your odours are like apples,[101] that is, your examples are imitable like those of the apostles. *Your throat is like the best wine.* The teaching of the Law is good wine; the instruction of the Gospel is better wine, but the infusion of the Holy Spirit is the best wine. The throat of the Virgin is her teaching, inspired by the Holy Spirit, which is like a wine to drink, that is, pleasing to imitate. And thus she said: *He has scattered the proud, he has exalted the humble* (Lk. 1:51,52).

She welcomes his praises saying: *Worthy* it is *for my beloved* to do this, namely to spare the subject and weaken the proud. *And for his lips and teeth to ruminate.* The lips of God are those who reveal his will; his teeth are those who trample vices. By them the doctrine of the Virgin is ruminated, that is, passed into memory, because *God resists the proud, but to the humble he gives grace* (I Petr 5:6).

In the following words the Virgin recalls those things she has done for the Church which will be converted from the Jews.

I have poured out prayers *to my beloved* for you, *and his turning to me,* that is, through me he wanted to turn to you in mercy. And thus I said: *Come my beloved,* to the Synagogue, out of mercy, since you fled from it on account of its fault of perfidy. *Let us go forth* by faith *into the field,* namely, into the whole world; *let us abide* by works *in the villages*, that is, among all peoples. *Let us get up early to the vineyards*, that is, to the synagogues of the Jews, which is to say, let us bring it about as soon as possible that the final moment shine in their hearts. *Let us see if the vineyards flourish*, that is, let us make them see in their minds how the Church has flourished in faith. *If the flowers be ready to bring forth fruits*, that is, let us see how they have become known through good works, and *if the pomegranates flourish*, that is, let us see how they have become[102] renowned through martyrdom. *There will I give you my breasts*, that is, they will imitate my example unto your honour. Note that "if" is said three times, which means that if they see thus and such in their heart,[103] they will imitate them in thought, word and deed.

The mandrakes, that is the heathens,[104] who like the mandrakes were without their Godhead, *give forth a smell* of good works *in our gates*, that is, in their virtues. And because now the fullness of the gentiles has come in, now is the time for eternal Isræl to be saved.[105] And so [515] *all the fruits, the new and the old, my beloved, I have kept for you*, which is to say: when they are converted, the Jews will keep the precepts of the Old and New Testaments unto your honour.

CHAPTER VIII

Who shall give you to me for my brother? born of the people of Judea, *sucking the breasts of my mother*, that is, taught in the Synagogue under the Law, *that I might find you without*, that is, I might see you being worshipped by the Jews who are thus far outside the faith, *and kiss you*, that is, that I might perceive you being loved by them. *And now no man may despise me*, namely, there will be no one of the Jews who will not believe that I remained a Virgin. *I will take hold of you,* that is, I will prove that you took flesh of me without the seed of man, *and bring you* through faith *into my mother's house,* that is, into the body of the Synagogue itself, *and into the chamber of her that conceived me,*[106] that is, into the understanding of Jewish law. *There you shall teach me* that you will be worshipped by them and that they will keep the precepts of the Lord. *And I will give you a cup,* that is, in imitation of me, they will offer you a good work of *spiced wine,* namely, of wisdom and charity, intoxicating others who drink it, *and a new wine of my pomegranates,* that is, a divine service filled with virtues. *His left hand under my head,* that is, they will despise temporal things for Christ, who is my head, *and his right hand shall embrace me,* that is, they shall seek only heavenly things, stimulated by him himself.

The Son speaks in favour of the Mother to the recently converted Church of the Jews.

I adjure you, O daughters of Jerusalem, that you stir not up the beloved, that is, that you feel nothing adverse of my mother the Virgin. This is repeated for the third time, that they may learn how much veneration is owing to God's mother.

There follows the praise of the Church converted from the Jews, wondering at the glory of the Virgin.

Who is this, that is, how great is her praise?[107] Rather, how worthy and virtuous is she *who comes up from the desert* of the world *flowing with delights* of heaven, *leaning upon her beloved,* that is, so exalted above the choirs of angels!

*The Son recounts to his Mother
the wickedness of the Jews
and alludes to their future conversion.*

Under the apple tree I raised you up, that is, redeeming you on the cross, I raised you above the heavens. *There your mother was corrupted,* namely, while crucifying me, Synagoga cursed herself with her own mouth when she said: *His blood be upon us and upon our children* (Matt 27:25). *There she was deflowered that bore you,* that is, they twisted the law which says: *The just you shall not kill* (Dan 13:53). But now, however, because with all their heart they turn to me, I say to them: *Put me as a seal upon your heart,* that is, imprint my image upon their hearts by love, *as a seal upon your arm,* that is, imprint my example through your acts. *For love is strong as death,* that is, just as formerly they deserved death because of their infidelity, now let them find life because of their love. *Jealousy is as hard as hell,* that is, just as earlier they plummeted into hell because of their harshness, so now they will enter into heaven because they have repented of their sins.[108] *The lamps thereof are lamps of fire and flames,*[109] that is, those among them who have charity will be glowing with the fire of the Holy Spirit, and shining with good works. I say to you that *many waters,* that is, the delights [516] or riches of the world *cannot extinguish their charity; neither can floods,* that is, all sorts of tribulations, *drown it. If a man should give all the substance of his house for love, he shall despise it as nothing,* that is, if anyone should offer them all the glory of the world, it could not separate them from the love of Christ.

*There follows the solicitude of the Virgin
for the Church of the Jews.*

Our sister Synagoga, who will be joined with us in the heritage of our father through faith, numbered among our citizens,[110] *is little, and has no breasts,* that is, she has no preachers[111] from which she may take examples for living. *What shall we do to our sister in the day when she is to be spoken to?* That is, what will become of Synagoga in the time when there will be preaching by Enoch and Elias?[112]

The Consolation of Christ to the Virgin.

If she be a wall, let us build upon it, that is, I will build her up in virtues like a wall, defended against vice on all sides. And I will do this *by bulwarks of silver,* that is, by the Scriptures which shine forth in eloquence. *If she be a door,* that is, let me make her a door for others by her example, that through her they may enter unto life. *Let us join it together with boards of cedar,* that is, I will adorn her with spiritual lilies.

The Promise of the Virgin.

I will be *a wall* for them, because if they imitate my life, they will be unconquerable by vice, *and* my[113] *breasts are as a tower,* that is, through my examples they will be safe in goodness. *Since I am become in his presence as one finding peace,* that is, from the time when I appeased him with prayers on their behalf and obtained for them his peace and grace, this prayer was answered, because *the peaceable* one, namely, Christ, *had a vineyard,* because the true vine, as the offspring of the blessed, willed to be begotten in me, *in that which had people,* that is, in my people, which brought forth the humble ones, namely, the apostles.[114] *He let out the same to keepers,* that is, he entrusted this people to the apostles, saying: *Go ye not into the way of the gentiles . . . but go ye rather to the lost sheep of the house of Israel* (Matt 10:5). Or else this means that he entrusted his vineyard to keepers, when hanging on the cross he said: *Behold your mother* (John 19:27), because afterward,[115] the other apostles [not just John] provided necessary things for her. *Every man brings for the fruit thereof a thousand pieces of silver,* that is, everyone of the faithful gives all that he has in order to gain Christ, the fruit of this vine.

Christ to the Faithful.

My vineyard is before me, that is, my mother stands in my glory. *A thousand are for you, the peaceable,* that is, many will be shoots springing from me, the vine, shooting up through faith, and imitating you in chastity, and because of this they will inherit life in peace, rejoicing. *And two hundred [pieces of silver] for them that keep the fruit thereof,* that is, those who preserve me, the fruit of life, through good works, will have a twofold reward.

Christ to the Virgin.[116]

You that dwell in the gardens, that is, now, O Mother, you will be venerated by both, *the friends hearken,* that is, all of the elect who imitate you, obey me. Now *make me hear your voice,* that is, make known what you most desire. [517]

Here follows the supplication of the Virgin for the separation of the just from the wicked.

You who in this life up until now[117] were hidden among the good and the evil, now *flee away* from evil ones, *O my beloved, and be like to the roe,* who knows good grasses from bad; so in your judgment, separate the damned from the elect. *And be like to the young hart,* who rests in the shade; so, too, turning away from the chaff, rest among the grain. And do this *upon the mountains of aromatical spices,* that is, above the height of the angels and men[118] who are mountains and aromatical spices, because among them you are all things in all, of high merit, of fragrant reward. This is what is to be said concerning the Canticle.[119]

*Now let us add a few things more
in honour of the Virgin.*

But because it is written: *Praise is not seemly in the mouth of a sinner* (Ecclus 15:9), I do not presume to praise the Mother of the Creator with polluted lips. Indeed, the sanctifier and lover of sanctity himself has shown how worthy she is of praise, he who judged her worth by virtue of her nature and chose to be born from the Virgin. And the reason was clear to all. Because just as death entered through a virgin woman, so life had to enter through a virgin woman. And there was another cause.

God made men in four ways: from earth, as with Adam; from man alone, as with Eve; from man and woman, as with us; and he made Christ from woman alone, a privilege which he kept for himself.[120] He wanted to be born from this sacred virgin and not others because she was the first in the world to pledge the vow of virginity.[121] But why did he not take her up with him when he ascended into the heavens, but left her here on earth for two years to be an example for the faithful? This is the reason: so that in his absence, she might be tested in sorrow, as gold in fire, so that afterwards she might shine forth more excellent than the angels, and so the heavens might exalt with new joy when the heavenly citizens would come forth festively to greet their queen, the Mother of God.

Her Nativity was not formerly celebrated, but being divinely revealed, it is preached that it should be celebrated in this manner. There was a hermit of holy life who every year heard harmony in heaven the night of her birth. When he marveled that he did not hear it at any other time, he began to ask God what it meant. The angels of the Lord appeared to him and they related these things to him: The perpetual Virgin who bore God was born this night. Although this was unknown to humankind, it is celebrated by the angels in heaven. Which revelation having been divulged, the celebration of her Nativity was instituted by the Church.[122]

And there are two reasons why the custom came to grow that flowers and grasses are consecrated on her festival. One, because her feast day[123] is adorned with flowers, since on this day it is sung concerning her: *They will surround her with flowers of roses and lilies of the valley.*[124] By roses we understand martyrs, and by lilies we understand virgins, by other flowers or herbs we understand the saints, each of whom is fragrant in goodness. The blessed Mother of God was a virgin and a martyr. Although she is glorified very much by all of the saints in general, nonetheless she is believed to be especially glorified by the virgins and martyrs. There is another cause: because all new fruits must be blessed before they are eaten, and this is barely observed in monasteries, the Church established that on her feast the first fruits would be blessed by the priests.

And two reasons occur to us why a procession should be held on this day. First, because on that day her most holy little body[125] was brought to burial with a procession of apostles and [518] other disciples of Christ. Secondly, because her most blessed spirit was borne into heaven by angels, in procession with the Son of God. Her body was revived afterwards, and is believed to have been gathered up into the glory of heaven.

The fact that the Church carries candles in their hands on her feast [that is, Candlemas, or Purification] is taken from the rite of the gentiles.[126] The empire of the Romans subjugated to itself the whole world, so that a census of all peoples was rendered to the Romans. And when these people had come, they would illuminate the city with lights in honour of their gods (who, of course, were demons), because they had subjugated the world to themselves, as they supposed. And there is a reason why they did this in February, under the sign of Aquarius. The sign of Aquarius is opposite the sign of Leo. For there are six signs, set opposite six others. The philosophers said that souls were made in eternity and are assigned to appropriate stars. When these had seen from on high the little bodies procreated within their mothers, they desired to be embodied, and because of this desire, they fell down from the heavens. The philosophers furthermore dogmatised that there were two gates of the heavens: one in the sign of Cancer through which souls will go out, the other in the sign of Capricorn, through which they will return. And when the souls going out through Cancer have arrived at Leo, there they began to descend opposite Aquarius and thus they wander through all the planets and in this manner they are embodied. But after they left the body, they had to return back through the kingdom of Pluto,[127] namely, of shadows, Pluto also being venerated in the same month. Thus arriving in Aquarius, they would receive their original dignity and through Capricorn enter the appropriate stars. Therefore, with this intention, they carried lights, so that after death[128] they might have bright passage through the place of shadow. This indeed they did, deceived by error. But we have spiritual authority by divine command. The whole world is subject to Christ's empire, and a census of divine service is rendered by all.

A candle is a figure of Christ, because just as bees reproduce without sexual union, so did the Virgin give birth without the embrace of man. Moreover, a candle, the work of bees, is formed in the shape of a column, because Christ, born of a virgin, was prophesied to be a finely–polished column of light to the blessed. A candle burns and shines because, in the judgment of Christ, the impious will burn with his majesty and the just will shine.[129] In a candle, three things are to be considered: flame, wax, wick.

the flame shines, the wax melts, and the wick, being enflamed, vanishes. All these things signify Christ. The light is his divinity, as is said: *I am the light of the world* (Jn. 8:12). The wax is his humanity, as likewise he said: *I am poured out like wax*.[130] The wick is his mortality, which is consumed in the fire of his Passion, as Simeon understood in Christ, therefore, exulting, he said, bearing him in his hands: *A light to the revelation of the Gentiles and the glory of thy people Israel* (Lk. 2:32). For this signification the Church carries lights in their hands on that day, so that with the five virgins,[131] the light of virtue being kindled by the five senses, after the death of the flesh, the Church deserves to escape the kingdom of darkness, and through the brightest star, Mary the Mother of God, they may see the light of Christ through the light of the Father.

Therefore, with devout praises, celebrate the Queen of Heaven, that she may eternally intercede on your behalf with her Son, the King of Angels, so that after this wretched pilgrimage you may reign with her through all eternity. Amen.

END NOTES

INTRODUCTION

[1] *PL* 172, 1110, translation from Sanford, p. 399.

[2] "Sub quinto Henrico floruit. Quis post hunc scripturus sit, posteritas videbit," *PL* 172, 232–34.

[3] "Sæpius rogato a condiscipulis," *PL* 172, 1109.

[4] "Fratres Cantuarensis ecclesiæ," *PL* 172, 813.

[5] Flint identified specific sources for the *Sigillum* and the *Speculum ecclesiæ* among manuscripts at Worcester. See "Career," pp. 75–80.

[6] Bauerreiss, "Honorius und Kuno."

[7] An exchange of letters between the two accompanied a late revision of the *Imago mundi* and their friendship was noted in the *Annales Palidenses*. Christian who was also the recipient of Honorius's lengthy and magisterial work on the Psalms. See Endres, p. 4.

[8] Endres, p. 60.

[9] Flint, "Chronology," pp. 233–234.

[10] "Nobilis henrici cuius pereunt inimici." See Flint, "Career," pp. 73–80. The closely related house at Lambach, which now possesses many of the manuscripts in that list, probably received the original bequest.

[11] Flint, "Heinricus of Augsburg."

[12] Honorius himself uses Augustodunensis to mean Autun in his biography of Reticius of Autun, copied from Jerome *De luminaribus, PL* 172, 206.

[13] M.–O. Garrigues, in *Positions des thèses* (Paris, 1967).

[14] See Endres and Sanford for other evidence and usages.

[15] Bauerreis, "Herkunft," presents convincing arguments for this interpretation.

[16] See Bauerreis, "Honorius and Kuno." pp. 311–312.

[17] See Southern, *St. Anselm*, pp. 209–217 and Reynolds.

[18] *PL* 172, 541.

[19] *PL* 172, 1197.

[20] *PL* 172, 494.

[21] One standard evaluation of Honorius based on the late dating is promoted by Ohly, *Hohelied–Studien*, pp. 251–54, and refuted by Flint, "Commentaries."

[22] Matter's insightful study *The Voice of My Beloved* is the first to explore some of the implications of the early date and assign credit for fluid and original analysis to Honorius.

[23] "Cantica canticorum exposuit, ita ut prius exposita non videantur." *PL* 172, 234.

[24] Honorius's disbelief in the Immaculate Conception obviously caused problems in this regard. For example, in the early thirteenth century, a scribe at Wilhering deleted an offending line of the *Sigillum* in his copy.

[25] Flint, "Place and Purpose," p. 109.

[26] Solomon appears both by name in 1:4, 3:7 and 3:9 and by epithet "the peaceable one" in Cant 8:11.

[27] Pope, p. 117.

[28] The homily is falsely attributed to St. Anselm in Migne, *PL* 158, cols. 644–649. Ralph d'Escures was exiled in England *ca.* 110, became Bishop of Rochester in 1108 and Archbishop of Canterbury in 1114. See Flint, "Chronology," p. 220.

[29] *PL* 158, 585–592. The true author of this is not securely

identified, although Flint suggests that he, too, is Ralph d'Escures. See "Commentaries," pp. 200–201.

[30] Flint, "Chronology," p. 200, n. 7, has identified these sources in detail.

[31] For example, the miracle of the Jewish boy is cited by Gregory of Tours and Paschasius Radbertus. See Flint, "Comentaries," p. 201–202; R.W. Southern, "English Origins."

[32] *PL* 30, 126–136. Some of the authority of this work may be due to the fact that it circulated under the name of St. Jerome.

[33] The present positions of the Church can be found in the bulls *Ineffabilis Deus* from Pius IX (1854) on the Immaculate Conception, and *Munificentissimus Deus* from Pius XII (1950) on the Assumption of Mary.

[34] *PL* 172, 479: "Sigillo est imago insculpta, quæ ceræ impressæ imaginem reddit. Sigillum est Christi humanitas, cui imago insculpta est Christi divinitas; cera vero humana anima, ad imaginem Dei formata." See Matter, p. 75.

[35] See the list in Flint,"Place and Purpose," pp. 125–126. To these can be added Wilhering IX, 110 (late 12th–early 13th c.) and the Augsburg Universitätsbibliothek 1 2 2° 13. Matter, p. 83, n. 67.

[36] Menhardt, "Mandragora," p. 178.

TEXT

[1] Mss VS, A, Va and K read *Fratres ad solitario*, "Brothers to the Hermit."

[2] See Ps 83:8 (Hebrew Psalter).

[3] See Matt 20:1–16.

⁴ See Matt 21:19.

⁵ See Ps 51:10.

⁶ See John 14:2.

⁷ Reading *pueritia namque regno* for *pueritia*, as in mss VS, A, K and Va.

⁸ See Luke 2:7.

⁹ Usually the mediæval exegetes understood the Mary of Luke 10:38 to be Mary Magdalene, although Honorius here seems to equate her with the Virgin Mary.

¹⁰ Reading *Filius suus* for *Filius*, as in mss VS, A, K, I and W.

¹¹ Reading *autem lectio* for *autem*, as in all HMML mss.

¹² Reading *electis* for *electas*, as in mss VS, K, I, Vb, and W.

¹³ Reading *in Jerusalem* for *Jerusalem*, as in mss VS, A, I, K and W.

¹⁴ Reading *cedrus* for *cedri*.

¹⁵ The name Libanus (Lebanon) is derived from the Hebrew root "to be white," either because the peak is covered in snow or because it is composed of light limestone. Since the recruits for military service in late Roman period were clothed in white, *candidatus* refers to a candidate for military service, or for any office. For Tertullian, "candidates of God" are those seeking baptism, so that in Christian terminology, *candidatus* refers to whiteness of the newly baptised or the stainless martyrs, washed clean and bright.

¹⁶ Inserting *dum semel aruit vitiis et concupiscentiis* for *cum semel aruit sicut ficus*, as in all HMML mss.

¹⁷ In Greek in the text, meaning "bearer of God," a title given to Mary at the Council of Ephesus in 431.

[18] Reading *longe majorem* for *majorem,* as in mss VS, A, K, I, Vb, and W.

[19] All HMML mss read *virgo odor cynamomi,* "the Virgin was the odour of cinnamon."

[20] Reading *in reges et sacerdotes* for *in rege,* as in all HMML mss. Honorius refers here to the ecclesiastical rituals of baptism and the consecration of priests and kings.

[21] Compare II Petr 1:4.

[22] Mss A, K, Va, I, and Vb read *Ecclesiæ Mater,* "Mother of the Church."

[23] Compare the *Regina coeli:* "For he whom you deserved to bear . . . ."

[24] The reference here is not clear, but the story of Mary of Egypt is often included among the Miracles of the Virgin, as in the collections of Dominic and William of Malmesbury. See Flint, "Commentaries," p. 201.

[25] Reading *vorticem cocyti* for *vertice,* as in all HMML mss. Cocytus, meaning "wailing" or "sorrow," names one of the rivers of the ancient underworld. It could mean hell in general, or specifically evoke the doom of the greedy. For Dante it was the ninth and bottom–most circle of Hell.

[26] Cedar refers to a Bedouin tribe of north Arabia, descended from one of the sons of Ishmæl (Gen 25:13). The word derives from the Hebrew for "swarthy" and the Cedarenes appear in the Bible as enemies of Isræl and haters of peace (Ps 119).

[27] Honorius explicates in the singular, although it is in the plural in the text.

[28] Honorius here refers to the Christological heresies which arose before the Council of Ephesus in 431 in which the orthodox statement on Christ's human and divine natures was decided. The first mistake was made by the

Docetists who felt that Jesus was a "divine phantom" whose body was not real, but appearance only, from the Greek *dokeo*, "I appear." The second contention might have been made by Arians who stressed that Christ was only a human, or by those who doubted the virgin birth.

[29] Reading *in qua* for in *quam*.

[30] Is 11:1. The rods *[virga]* of Moses (Ex 17:1–7; Num 20:1–13) and Jesse (Is 11:1) were often compared to Mary the Virgin *[virgo]*. During the twelfth century, the family tree of Jesse, culminating in the Virgin and Christ became one of the most enduring images of Christ's fulfillment of Old Testament prophecy.

[31] We follow the Douay–Rheims here in translating the female *amica* of the Canticle "love" and the male *dilectus* as the "beloved."

[32] Inserting the text Canticle 1:16.

[33] Reading *Tigna* for *Ligna*, in accordance with the Canticle text. Honorius then lists the four cardinal virtues, known from ancient times.

[34] Both the Migne text and the HMML mss omit lines here, so the chapter has been ended and Canticle text inserted, in more orderly fashion.

[35] Reading *absque* for *ab*. Compare Luke 1:35.

[36] Reading *velit, id est sicut ipsa velit* for *velit*, as in mss VS, A, K, Va, Vb, and W.

[37] All HMML mss read *per fenestras*, "born through windows," for *de Virgine*.

[38] Reading *confidens* for *confidentes*, as in all HMML mss.

[39] Honorius changes the text by substituting *nos* for *vos*.

[40] Inserting *sed*, as in all HMML mss.

[41] Reading *montes, id est fac eos illorum confortes qui fuerunt montes Bethel* for *montes*, as in all HMML mss. Bether, appearing only in the Canticle, seems to name "mountains of separation," probably peaks which are cleft or rugged. Honorius blithely reads here the more common *Bethel* which means "House of God."

[42] Reading *intelligere* for *intellige*, as in mss VS, A, K, Vb, and W.

[43] Compare Mt. 11:27.

[44] Reading *Christus ad doctores de Virginis* for *Corpus de virginis ad doctores*, as in all HMML mss.

[45] Ms K reads simply "on the Assumption of Mary."

[46] The name Solomon means "peacemaker."

[47] Inserting *Sequitur*, as in all HMML mss.

[48] Compare Matt 6:22.

[49] Mt. Galaad (Gilead) means "heap of witness," as in Gen 31:41–52, the "witness heap" or the "hillock of testimony" between Laban and Jacob.

[50] Reading *inhianter* for *inhiante*, as in mss VS, A, and I.

[51] Compare I Cor 13:12.

[52] Reading *myrra, scilicet amari in passione altitudo* for *myrra, id est altitudo*, as in mss. A, K, Vb, and W.

[53] Inserting *quia hostia dei celsitudo*, as in mss A, K, Va, I, Vb, and W.

[54] Ms K reads *sponsalis*, emphasising the marriage imagery. Another translation of *triclinium* in the preceding line would be "bedchamber."

[55] Honorius writes *monte Amana* for the Vulgate *capite Amana*. Amana means "faith" or "steadfastness", but Honorius may be thinking instead of Aman, the enemy of the Jews in Est 3:1–10.

[56] Sanir is the Amorite name of Mt. Hermon, in the southern end of the Anti–Lebanon chain, a source of rich blessings according to Prov 25:13 and Ps 132:3.

[57] The Vulgate reads *unguentorum*, but *vestimentorum* is a variation noted by Pope.

[58] Reading *operum* for *uberum*, as in all HMML mss.

[59] *Signaculum*, a seal, might also be translated as "sign," as, for example, circumcision is a *signaculum fides*, a "sign of faith."

[60] Reading *ut unguentum* for *unguento*, as in mss VS, A, K, I, Vb, and W.

[61] Honorius here omits a line of the Canticle from his commentary.

[62] Reading *se invenire* for in *se venire*, as in mss VS, I, and Vb.

[63] Reading *quod* for *quo*.

[64] All HMML mss read *hominibus* for *omnibus*.

[65] For *rore* reading *rore, id est qui in patrem credunt pleni sunt errore*, as in mss VS, A, K, Va, Vb, and I.

[66] See Prov 26:11.

[67] Douay–Rheims here translates *venter* as "bowels," although it might also mean "belly" or "womb."

[68] Reading *hec opera* for *opera* as in mss VS, A, I, Vb, K, and W.

[69] This methodological comment alludes to the speculative grammar, or logic, which provides the basis of the scholastic method.

[70] For *ingreditur* reading *ingressus patuit*, as in all HMML mss.

[71] Inserting *ipsa*, as in all HMML mss.

[72] Reading *non inveni* for *inveni*, as in all HMML mss.

[73] Inserting *eum*, as in mss VS, Vb and W.

[74] Reading *tuus* for *meus*, as in Mss VS, A, I, Vb and W.

[75] Reading *sic verbo* for *verbo*, as in all HMML mss.

[76] Reading *omnibus* for *hominibus*, as in all HMML mss.

[77] Compare Is 11:2–3.

[78] Compare Augustine, *Confessions*, Book 1, chap. 1.

[79] Reading *id est in Ecclesiam ad areolam aromatis, scilicet qui in se colligunt virtutes* for *id est Ecclesiam, ut colligat virtutes*, as in all HMML mss.

[80] Reading *quia ascendunt* for *ascendentes* as in mss A, K, Vb and W.

[81] The Douay–Rheims translates *cortex* as "bark."

[82] Reading *mores* for *mones*, as in mss VS, A, K, I, Vb, and W.

[83] See Mt. 25:35–40.

[84] See Mt. 5:3–12.

[85] Honorius reads *matri suæ*, a variation listed by Weber.

[86] Honorius reads *genetrici* as "for her" rather than "of her" as in Douay–Rheims.

[87] For *per partum* all HMML mss read *perpetua*, the perpetual Virgin.

[88] Reading *qui nobis* for *quando* as in mss VS, A, I, K, and W.

[89] Reading *utrum* for *ut*.

[90] For *ipsa docuit me facere* reading *impedivit me scire*, as in all HMML mss.

[91] *Exhortatio virginis* added in all HMML mss.

[92] Honorius reads "they" for "we" in this last passage.

[93] Reading *clavo* for *clivo*, as in all HMML mss.

[94] For *uberibus*, all HMML mss read *umbilico*, the navel or umbilical cord, emphasising the physical process of birth.

[95] This text, unclear both in Migne and HMML mss, has been rearranged and a variation of the Douay–Rheims passage inserted for clarity.

[96] Reading *brachiis* for *brachio*, as in all HMML mss.

[97] The references in Cant 7:4 are to otherwise unknown topographical features of Hesebon (Heshbon), the ancient royal city of the Amorites. Bat-Rabbim, which the Douay–Rheims renders as "the gate of the daughter of the multitude" is now considered a proper name of uncertain meaning.

[98] Inserting *de imis*, as in all HMML mss.

[99] See Num 13:25.

[100] Compare Is 63:2–3.

[101] Honorius reads *odores tui*, which Weber lists as a variation of *odor oris tui*.

[102] After *quomodo* inserting *bona opera protulerunt. Si floruerunt mala punica, id est, faciamus eos videre quomodo* as in mss VS, A, K, I,Vb and W.

[103] For *viderint* reading *corde viderint*, as in all HMML mss.

[104] Reading *gentiles* for *gentilitas*, as in mss VS, A, I, Vb, and W.

[105] Compare Rom 11:25–27.

[106] This phrase does not appear in the Vulgate, although it is part of Hebrew and LXX versions.

[107] Reading *ista quanta est laude* for *quanta*, as in ms VS and I.

[108] For *emendationem vitiorum intrabunt*, all HMML mss read *emulationem meliorum intrent*, "because they have

emulated better things."

[109] Honorius here deviates slightly from the Douay–Rheims.

[110] For *nostrorum civium*, all HMML mss read *credentium*, "believers."

[111] Reading *predicatores* for *predicationem*, as in Mss VS, A, K, I and W.

[112] The two witnesses of Apoc 11:3–12 are usually identified as Enoch and Elijah, who are to return to accomplish the conversion of the Jews before the end of the world. See also Mal 4:5, Matt 11:4, 17:10–12.

[113] Reading *mea* for *tua*, as in mss VS, A, K, I, Vb and W.

[114] In this passage, the Vulgate translates the proper noun Baalhamon into a phrase of obscure meaning, which Honorius further obscures.

[115] Inserting *postea*, as in mss VS, A, K, I, Vb, and W.

[116] Adding *Christus ad Virginem*, as in mss VS, A, K, I, Vb, and W.

[117] Adding *hactenus*, as in mss VS, A, K, I, Vb, and W.

[118] Reading et *hominum qui* for *inter eos qui*, as in mss VS, A, K, Va, Vb, and W.

[119] This marks the end of the *Sigillum* proper. Ms. I does not continue.

[120] See Anselm, *Cur Deus homo*, c. VIII. Compare also Honorius, *Elucidarius*, PL 172, 1122.

[121] After *privilegium*, all HMML mss add *Quid ab hac Virgine sacra non ab alia nasci voluit, quæ ipsa prima in mundo votum virginitate vovit*.

[122] There is no significantly older source for this miracle, also mentioned by Anselm (*Oratio* VII), and repeated by Honorius in the *Speculum Ecclesiæ PL* 172, 1001. See Flint,

"Commentaries," p. 202. In *The Golden Legend* under September 8, Nativity of Mary, credited to John Beleth. This event resembles the legend of Helsinus, who was urged by a vision of St. Peter to institute the Feast of the Immaculate Conception, specifically using the liturgy of the Nativity.

[123] For *festivitas*, Mss VS, A, K, Vb, and W read *sollempnitas*.

[124] This is the antiphonal response for the first Nocturn of the Office of the Assumption.

[125] The question of whether Mary truly died and the distinction between the rising of Mary's soul and her body were important points in the debate over the Immaculate Conception. The mss offer several variants. Reading here *corpusculum illa die* as in A, K, Vb, and W for Migne's *corpus vel illa* ("her body, rather, she herself"). In VS, and Va, *corpuscula illa die*.

[126] Compare Honorius, *Speculum ecclesiæ*, PL 172, 852; and *Sacramentarium*, PL 172, 798. Such theories about the celestial afterlife of souls were common in the ancient world.

[127] Ms K reads Plato for Pluto.

[128] Reading *post mortem* for *postmodum*, as in mss VS, A, K, Vb, and W.

[129] All HMML mss. insert the following before *cereus: Ideo autem cereus Christi figuram gerit, quia sicut apes absque soitu gignit, ita virgo sine virile complexu genuit. Cereus autem opus apis in modum collune formature quia Christus natus virginis teres colluna lucis beatorum predicatur. Cereus ardet et lucet quia de judicio Christi impii ardent de maiestate et justi lucent.*

[130] Compare Ps 21:15.

[131] See Mt. 25:1–13. In the parable, the five wise virgins,

who have prepared their lamps against the darkness, represent the elect who are joined to Christ the bridegroom at the end of time.